# China
# A B C

NEW WORLD PRESS
Beijing, China

**ISBN 0-8351-1393-0**

*Published by*
NEW WORLD PRESS
24 Baiwanzhuang Road, Beijing, China

*Distributed by*
CHINA INTERNATIONAL BOOK TRADING CORPORATION
(Guoji Shudian)
P.O. Box 399, Beijing, China

*Printed in the People's Republic of China*

## EDITOR'S NOTE

Our aim in publishing this book is to present the reader with a comprehensive, up-to-date survey of China as it is today, encompassing both the richness of the nation's ancient cultural heritage as well as the situation in the modern day socialist state, that is, the People's Republic of China.

Because of the broadness of the scope of this book, we have at times been forced to sacrifice a certain depth for the sake of comprehensiveness. Since it was necessary to limit each essay to a certain length, the treatment of each subject has perforce been rather drastically capsulized. This condensation has necessitated the foregoing of a certain fineness of detail, no thoroughgoing analysis of each subject being possible within the limited space available to us. Indeed, the majority of the book's 57 articles would be sufficient to serve as the subjects of entire books in their own right. Nevertheless, the radically condensed nature of the material in this book also has a strong point: it makes *China ABC* an ideal handbook for all those who wish to get better acquainted with China at a glance, without wading through dense pages of technical material.

This book will prove itself an indispensable companion not only to those intending to go sightseeing, do business or study in the People's Republic, but to anyone who wishes within the space of a few hour's reading to gain a vivid sense of all those things that are unique to China, and the singularity of its contribution to world civilization.

# CONTENTS

# THE ORIGIN OF THE NAME OF THE PEOPLE'S REPUBLIC OF CHINA

With more than four thousand years of recorded history, China is the cradle of one of the world's oldest civilizations. In ancient times, the Xia tribe* established a state in the area of the Huanghe River (Yellow River) basin. The tribesmen, believing that this was the center of the world, called this state the Middle Kingdom and regarded the surrounding areas as being peripheral. China has been known by this name even after the 1911 Revolution, which abolished the feudal monarchy and gave birth to the Republic of China. However, the establishment of the Republic of China did not mark the completion of the Chinese people's historical task of combating feudalism and imperialism.

In 1949, after a long and arduous struggle, the Chinese Communist Party under the leadership of Chairman Mao Zedong led the Chinese people of all nationalities to finally overthrow the rule of imperialism, feudalism and bureaucratic capitalism, gaining victory for the new democratic revolution and establishing the People's Republic of China. From then on, the Chinese people took control of their country's fate and became its masters.

---

* An ancient legend has it that the earliest ancestors of the Han people were the Huang Di and Yan Di tribes, who lived in the region of the Huanghe River (Yellow River) basin. "Di" was originally the title of the tribal chief. Judging from archaeological evidence, they lived about 3000 B.C. After centuries of living side by side, the two tribes gradually melded into one, and by the time of the Xia dynasty (c. 21-16 centuries B.C.) they were known as the Hua Xia people. The nationality which is today known as the Han was itself formed over long generations of intermarriage between the Hua Xia and other peoples. Though at present the Chinese people are referred to as belonging to the Han nationality (the name generally considered to have been taken from the Han dynasty, 206 B.C.-220 A.D.), when tracing back their remotest origins they still refer to themselves as "the descendants of Yan and Huang".

From June 15 to June 19, 1949, the Preparatory Committee for the Chinese People's Political Consultative Conference (CPPCC)* held its first meeting in Beiping (as Beijing was called at the time) concerning the founding of the state. Because a name for the country had not yet been decided upon, it was temporarily called the People's Democratic Republic of China.

On September 18 of the same year, while making a report at the second meeting of the Preparatory Committee, Zhou Enlai started using the name the People's Republic of China.

From September 21-30, 1949, the First Chinese People's Political Consultative Conference was held in Beijing. In the meeting on September 22, Dong Biwu discussed the question of naming the country. He said, "We have chosen the name 'the People's Republic of China' because our political system is a republic.

---

* Before the National People's Congress was elected, the CPPCC temporarily functioned in its stead. After the NPC was elected in 1954, the CPPCC became a broadly representative United Front organization and today continues to participate in decision making on national policy and plays an important role in the democratic supervision of policy implementation.

Tian'anmen Square, the Center of Beijing

The word 'people' in the new democracy of today's China refers to the working class, the peasantry, the petty bourgeoisie and the national bourgeoisie. This is the precise definition. Since the word expresses the concept of a 'democratic dictatorship of the people', repeating the word 'democratic' is unnecessary." Thus the first meeting of the People's Political Consultative Conference officially chose the People's Republic of China as the country's name.

# THE NATIONAL FLAG OF THE PEOPLE'S REPUBLIC OF CHINA

The national flag of the People's Republic of China is the five star red flag. The face of the flag is red, the color of revolution, and its shape is rectangular, with the length of its sides in 3:2 proportion. In the upper left hand corner there are five yellow stars; one large star and four smaller stars in an arc. The diameter of the circumcircle of the large star measures three-tenths of the height of the flag, while the diameter of the circumcircles of the smaller stars is precisely one-tenth of the height. The tip of one corner of each of the smaller stars points directly towards the center of the large star which stands for the Communist Party of China. Collectively the five stars symbolize the great unity of the Chinese people under the Communist Party of China. The stars are yellow in color so that they will stand out clearly against the red background. The portion of the flag which is fitted over the flagpole is white. On June 19, 1949, the Preparatory Committee for the Chinese People's Political Consultative Conference organized a small group to select a national anthem and design the national flag and emblem. On July 18 of the same year, notices were placed in the newspapers soliciting designs for the flag and emblem and for words and lyrics for the national anthem. In August, the Appraisal Committee of the Preparatory Committee for the Chinese People's Political Consultative Conference (CPPCC) in conjunction with an advisory group selected 38 designs from a total of 4,912 and submitted them to the First Plenary Session of the CPPCC for discussion and approval. On September 27, 1949, it was resolved that the national flag of the People's Republic of China would be the Five Star Red Flag.

On October 1, 1949, Chairman Mao Zedong personally raised the first Five Star Red Flag in Tian'anmen Square. And each of the four constitutions adopted subsequently have clearly stipulated: the flag of the People's Republic of China is the Five Star Red Flag.

The flag was designed by the Shanghai economist Zeng Liansong (born 1927). He was not an artist by profession, but rather an economist engaged in economic planning and price adjustment. He executed the design for the flag just as he was preparing to start work in a Shanghai supply and marketing cooperative.

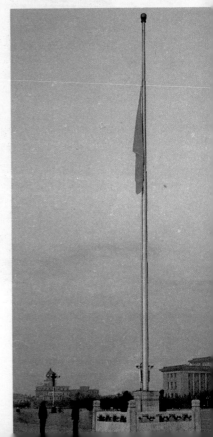

# THE NATIONAL EMBLEM OF THE PEOPLE'S REPUBLIC OF CHINA

Since 1954, all constitutions adopted by the People's Republic of China have stipulated: "The national emblem of the People's Republic of China depicts Tian'anmen in the center illuminated by five stars and encircled by ears of wheat and a cogwheel."

The Chinese people's new democratic revolution began with the May 4th Movement in 1919. Tian'anmen (the Gate of Heavenly Peace) was the birthplace of this movement, and the site of the founding ceremony of the People's Republic of China on October 1, 1949. At present, Tian'anmen Square stands as the geographical center of the Chinese capital, and has become the site most deeply cherished by all of China's nationalities. Therefore, the choice of Tian'anmen as a symbol for the national spirit is entirely appropriate: the cogwheel and ears of wheat stand respectively for the working class and peasantry, and the five stars representing the great alliance of the Chinese people under the leadership of the Chinese Communist Party.

Suggestions for the national emblem, national flag and national anthem were solicited publicly in newspaper announcements in 1949. After receiving 1,120 designs, the Selection Committee submitted several of the best ones to an Appraisal Committee which, working together with several artists, undertook to improve and combine these designs into a single design. Following several more discussions and alterations, today's national emblem finally emerged, and it was approved by the Second Session of the First Conference of the Chinese People's Political Consultative Conference (CPPCC), held from June 14 to 23 in 1950, which submitted it for adoption by the Central People's Government. Finally, on June 28, 1950, the Central People's Government formally adopted the design for the national emblem which had been put forward by the CPPCC.

# THE NATIONAL ANTHEM OF THE PEOPLE'S REPUBLIC OF CHINA

The national anthem of the People's Republic of China is *The March of the Volunteers.* It was first composed in 1935.

On June 15, 1949, the Preparatory Committee for the Chinese People's Political Consultative Conference decided to solicit songs suitable for China's national anthem and on July 18 it inserted notices in the newspapers to this effect. On September 27, 1949, the Preparatory Committee passed a resolution that until such time as a national anthem was officially chosen *The March of the Volunteers* would serve as a temporary anthem. During the "cultural revolution" there was a period when *The East Is Red* was used as a substitute national anthem. Later, the earlier national anthem was restored, though according to a resolution passed by the People's Congress in 1978, its lyrics were changed. In 1982, the Fifth Session of the Fifth National People's Congress resolved to restore the original 1935 version of *The March of the Volunteers* as the official national anthem.

*The March of the Volunteers* originally served as the theme song of the Chinese movie *Children of Turbulence.** It was written by the lyricist Tian Han** and the composer Nie Er*** in 1935. This was a time

---

* The movie *Children of Turbulence* is set in the war-torn China of the 1930s. It describes how intellectuals under Kuomintang rule were jolted out of their complacency by the Japanese occupation of the three northeastern provinces, and how they bravely took their places alongside their compatriots fighting at the front.

** Tian Han (1898-1968). In his youth, Tian Han studied in Japan, returning to China in 1921. In 1932, he joined the Chinese Communist Party. He was an active dramatist and poet, and wrote more than one hundred plays, operas and other dramatic works. His most celebrated works include *The White Snake, Guan Hanqing* and *Xie Yaohuan.*

*** Nie Er (1912-1935). Born the son of an impoverished doctor, Nie Er fell in love with music at an early age and mastered numerous folk instruments. He went to Shanghai in 1930, and the following year

# NATIONAL ANTHEM

(March of the Volunteers)

Music by Nie Er
Words by Tian Han

March Tempo, Vivace

of grave national peril, and as soon as the song appeared it was rapidly transmitted to every part of the country. *The March of the Volunteers* expresses the Chinese people's desire to resist foreign aggression and strengthen their nation; it conveys as well their revolutionary spirit, their staunchness in the face of violence and their willingness to lay down their lives for freedom and liberation.

---

joined the Mingyue Song and Dance Troupe as a violinist. In 1933, he joined the Chinese Communist Party. In 1935, shortly after composing *The March of the Volunteers*, he embarked on a trip to Russia via Japan. During his stopover in Japan, he drowned while swimming in Kanagawa County. His more than thirty songs include *The March of the Volunteers*, *The Graduation Song* and *The New Women*. He also adapted four folk melodies, including *The Mad Dance of the Golden Snake*.

# CHINA'S CONSTITUTION

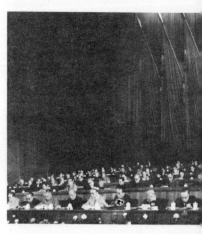

The Opening Session of the 2nd Plenum of the 6th NPC, 1984

The Plenum of the First Chinese People's Political Consultative Conference (CPPCC) was held in Beijing on September 21-30, 1949. On September 29, the conference ratified the Common Program of the CPPCC, which served as China's provisional constitution.

In late 1952, a decision was made to hold a national people's congress through general elections and to formulate an official constitution on the basis of the Common Program of the CPPCC. At its 43rd session held on December 24, 1952, the Standing Committee of the CPPCC National Committee decided to commence drafting the constitution, and

on January 13, 1953, a committee for this purpose was set up. A draft constitution was unanimously approved on June 14, 1954, at the 30th plenum of the Central People's Government Committee and submitted for national discussion. All Chinese nationalities took an active part in the discussions, and their comments and suggestions were studied carefully by the committee and revisions were made accordingly.

The revised draft was discussed and approved by the 34th plenum of Central People's Government Committee on September 9, 1954. On September 20 at the First Session of the First National People's Congress, this approv-

ed draft was passed by secret ballot and the first Chinese Constitution came into being. It includes a preamble and divided into 106 articles in four chapters.

The second Chinese Constitution was adopted by the Fourth National People's Congress at its first session on January 13, 1975. It contains only 30 articles with a completely rewritten preamble. During the First Session of the Fifth National People's Congress on March 5, 1978, the third Chinese Constitution was promulgated. It contains a preamble and divided into 60 articles in four chapters.

To prepare the fourth Constitution, a Committee to Amend the Constitution was established on September 10, 1980. A draft version was completed in February 1982, and later submitted for national discussion by the Standing Committee of the National People's Congress. On December 4, 1982, the present Constitution of the People's Republic of China was adopted by secret ballot by the Fifth Session of the Fifth National People's Congress. It includes a preamble and four chapters entitled "General Principles", "The Fundamental Rights and Duties of Citizens", "The Structure of the State", and "The National Flag, the National Emblem and the Capital".

# GEOGRAPHICAL LOCATION, AREA AND BOUNDARIES

CHINA'S ADMINISTRATIVE DIVISIONS

The People's Republic of China is located in the eastern part of the Eurasian Continent, on the west coast of the Pacific Ocean. The southeast portion of the country faces the ocean, while the northwest extends deep into the continent. From north to south, it stretches from Mohe town on the Heilong River on the northern border of Heilongjiang Province (Latitude 53° N.) to the Zengmu Reef of the Nansha Islands in the south (Latitude 4° N.), a total distance of 5,500 kilometers. From east to west, it stretches from the Pamir Mountains in the Xinjiang Uygur Autonomous Region in the west (Longitude 73° E.) to the confluence of the Heilong and Wusuli rivers in the east (Longitude 135° E.), a distance of 5,200 kilometers.

The third largest country in the world, China has a total land area of 9.6 million square kilometers. China has a land border more than 20,000 kilometers long and is bordered by 12 countries: the Democratic People's Republic of Korea, the People's Republic of Mongolia, the Soviet Union, Afghanistan, Pakistan, India, Nepal, Sikkim, Bhutan, Burma, Laos and Viet Nam.

The coastline extends more than 18,000 kilometers from the

mouth of the Yalu River on the Sino-Korean border to the mouth of the Beilun River on the Sino-Vietnamese border. From north to south, the Chinese mainland is flanked by the Bohai Gulf, the Huanghai Sea (Yellow Sea), and the East China and South China seas. China's neighbors in the surrounding seas are Japan, the Philippines, Brunei, Indonesia and Malaysia. More than 5,000 islands are scattered across China's vast territorial seas, the largest being Taiwan, with a total land area of 35,788 square kilometers. Hainan Island in Guangdong Province is the second largest, with a total surface area of 34,380 square kilometers, and Chongming Island of Shanghai is the third, with a surface area of 1,083 square kilometers. The numerous islands, islets, reefs and shoals dotting the South China Sea are subdivided into four basic groups: the Dongsha, the Xisha, the Zhongsha and the Nansha islands. The Nansha Islands lie at the southernmost extremity of China's territorial seas.

## THE HIGHEST PLATEAU IN THE WORLD

The Qinghai-Tibet Plateau in the southwest of China covers an area of 2.3 million square kilometers, or approximately 20 percent of the nation's total surface area. Having an average elevation of 4,000 meters above sea level, the Qinghai-Tibet Plateau is the world's highest, and as such is popularly known as the "roof of the world". It is the source of many of the rivers of East Asia, Southeast Asia and South Asia, has more than 100 big lakes, each with an average surface area of over 100 square kilometers, and has 10 mountain peaks which stand at an average of 8,000 meters above sea level.

# MAJOR MOUNTAINS

China is a mountainous country, with two-thirds of its surface area covered by mountains or hilly areas.

1. *East-West Mountain Ranges*

The Himalaya Mountains lie in the areas of China's Tibetan Autonomous Region, Pakistan, India, Nepal, Sikkim and Bhutan. It is the world's largest mountain chain and its peak, Mount Qomolangma, the highest mountain in the world, soars 8,848.13 meters above sea level on the Sino-Nepalese border.

The Karakorum Mountains start from the Xinjiang-Kashmir border in the northwest and stretch southeastwards into northern Tibet. The average height of the range is 6,000 meters above sea level, while the Qogir, its main peak, towers 8,611 meters above the Sino-Pakistani border, making it the second highest summit in the world.

The Kunlun Mountains start from the eastern Pamir plateau in the west, traverse the Xinjiang Uygur and Tibet autonomous regions, and extend into Qinghai Province in the east. The average height of the mountain range is 6,000 meters above sea level, though a number of its famous peaks, such as Kongur (7,719 meters), Kongurjiubie (7,595 meters) and Muztagata (7,555 meters), rise well above this height.

The Tianshan Mountains run through the middle of the Xinjiang Uygur Autonomous Region, dividing the area into north and south, while in the west they extend into Soviet Central Asia. The average height of the range is 3,000 to 5,000 meters above sea level. Its two main peaks are Mount Tomer (7,435 meters) and Mount Hantengri (6,995 meters), the latter being situated on the Sino-Soviet border.

The Gangdise Mountain Range traverses southwestern Tibet, and averages approximately 6,000 meters in height. Its main peak is Mount Kangrenboqi (6,714 meters).

The Altay Mountains are situated in the northern part of the Xinjiang Uygur Autonomous Region and western Mongolia, while in the north and west they extend into the Soviet Union. The average height of the range is 2,000 to 3,000 meters above sea level.

The Qinling Mountain Range extends 1,500 kilometers across central China, forming a natural geographical boundary between northern and southern China. Its main peak is Mount Taibai (3,767 meters).

## 2. Northeast-Southwest Mountain Ranges

The Changbai Mountains traverse the eastern portion of Liaoning, Jilin and Heilongjiang provinces as well as the northeastern section of the Sino-Korean border. Their elevation ranges from 200 to 2,000 meters above sea level and their main peak is Mount Baitou (2,744 meters).

The Greater Hinggan Mountains are situated in the northeast portion of the Inner Mongolia Autonomous Region and in eastern Heilongjiang Province. Their average elevation ranges from 1,100 to 1,400 meters, but some of the higher peaks in the range exceed 1,700 meters.

The Nanling Mountains, also known as the Five Mountains, includes all the mountains along the common borders of Guangxi, Guangdong, Hunan and Jiangxi provinces. It includes the Yuechengling, Dupang-ling, Mengzhuling, Qitianling and Dayuling mountains, along with the granite-peaked Jiulian Mountains, with a combined average height of 1,000 meters above sea level.

## 3. Northwest-Southeast Mountain Ranges

The Bayanhar Mountains are located in south-central Qinghai Province. Their elevation ranges from 5,000 to 6,000 meters in height and their main peak is Mount Yagradaze 5,442 meters).

The Qilian Mountains are situated in western Gansu and eastern Qinghai provinces and are formed of several parallel mountain ranges, Mount Qilian being at their northernmost point. The range averages more than 4,000 meters above sea level, while its tallest peaks rise considerably higher. They include Mount Lenglong (4,843 meters), Mount Qilian (5,547 meters) and Mount Shulenan (5,808 meters).

The Lesser Hinggan Mountains, also known as the Eastern Hinggan Range, is located in northern Heilongjiang Province and has an average height of 600 to 1,000 meters. Some of the summits in the chain were formerly active volcanoes. Mounts Huoshao and Laohei in Dedu County erupted in

1720, forming the Wudalian-chi lakes as a consequence.

### 4. *North-South Mountain Ranges*

The Hengduan Mountains are situated in western Sichuan and Yunnan provinces and extend into the eastern part of the Tibet Autonomous Region. Their average elevation ranges from 2,000 to 6,000 meters above sea level and their main peak is Mount Gongga (7,556 meters).

The Taiwan Mountains is the collective name for the Tai-dong Mountains, the Zhong-yang Mountains, the Yushan Mountains and the Ali Mountains. Among the principal peaks of these mountains are Mount Xingang (1,682 meters), Mount Xiuguluan (3,833 meters), Mount Data (2,663 meters), Mount Yushan (3,950 meters), the highest peak in Taiwan Province, and Mount Xueshan (3,884 meters), the second highest peak in Taiwan Province.

The Five Holy Mountains (Wu Yue) is the collective name for Mount Taishan in Shandong Province (1,545 meters), Mount Huashan in Shaanxi (2,154 meters), Mount Song-shan in Henan (1,512 meters), Mount Hengshan in Hunan (1,290 meters) and Mount Hengshan in Shanxi (2,016 meters). Chinese legend has it that these mountains are the gathering places of the gods and in past ages these were the places where Chinese emperors customarily offered sacrifices.

China's four principal Buddhist mountains are the Wutai Mountains in Shanxi (highest peak 3,058 meters), Mount Pu-tuo in Zhejiang (290 meters), Jiuhua Mountains in Anhui (Mount Tiantai is the principal peak, 1,341 meters) and Mount Emei in Sichuan (3,099 meters).

Mount Qomolangma, Main Peak of the Himalayas

# MAJOR RIVERS

China has numerous rivers, the majority of which flow from west to east and ultimately drain into the Pacific Ocean. Among these are the Changjiang (Yangtze) River, the Huanghe (Yellow) River, the Zhujiang (Pearl) River and the Huaihe River. Rivers which flow from north to south and drain into the Indian Ocean after passing beyond China's borders are the Yarlungzangbo and the Nujiang rivers. The Ertix River flows north, passing beyond China's borders to drain ultimately into the Arctic Ocean. Most of China's major inland rivers are located in the north and west, the most important being the Tarim River and the Chaidamu River. In addition, there are also man-made rivers such as the Grand Canal.

The Changjiang is China's longest river and the third longest in the world. Its source is the Tuotuo River, which originates on the southwestern slopes of Mount Geladandong, the main peak of the Tanggula Mountains, which joins with the Tongtian River and the Jinsha River to form the Changjiang. The river flows through Qinghai, Tibet, Sichuan, Yunnan, Hubei Hunan, Jiangxi, Anhui and Jiangsu, finally emptying into the East China Sea at Shanghai. Its principal tributaries are the Yalong River, the Minjiang River, the Jialing River, the Wujiang River, the Xiangjiang River, the Hanshui River, the Ganjiang River and the Huangpu River. It has a total length of 6,300 kilometers and a drainage area of more than 1,800,000 square kilometers.

The Huanghe is the second longest river in China. Originating at the northern foot of the Bayanhar Mountains in Qinghai Province, it traverses Qinghai, Sichuan, Gansu, Ningxia, Inner Mongolia, Shanxi, Shaanxi, and Henan before finally draining into the Bohai Gulf in Shandong Province. Its principal tributaries are the Taohe River, the Huanghe River, the Wuding River, the Fenhe River, the Weihe River, the Luohe River and the Qinhe River. It has a total length of

5,464 kilometers and a drainage area of 752,400 square kilometers.

The Heilong River is one of the great rivers of Asia. In the south, it originates as the Ergune River, passing through the western slopes of the Greater Hinggan Mountain Range, while in the north it begins as the Shilege River, arising at the eastern foot of Mount Kente in Mongolia. The Heilong River itself begins where these two rivers flow together west of Mohe town in Heilongjiang Province. From here until it joins the Wusuli River at Khabarovsk in the Soviet Union, the Heilong

One of the Picturesque Gorges Along the Changjiang River

## CHINA'S MAJOR RIVERS

| Name | Length (km) | Drainage Area (km²) | Province/Region It Traverses |
|---|---|---|---|
| Changjiang River (Yangtze River) | 6,300 | 1,800,000 | Qinghai, Sichuan, Tibet, Yunnan, Hubei, Hunan, Jiangxi, Anhui, Jiangsu, Shanghai |
| Huanghe River (Yellow River) | 5,464 | 752,400 | Qinghai, Sichuan, Gansu, Ningxia, Inner Mongolia, Shanxi, Shaanxi, Henan, Shandong |
| Heilong River | 4,350 (portion in Chinese territory measures 2,965) | 890,000 (in Chinese territory) | Heilongjiang |
| Zhujiang River (Pearl River) | 2,200 | 452,000 | Yunnan, Guizhou, Guangxi, Guangdong, Hunan, Jiangxi |
| Tarim River | 2,179 | 198,000 | Xinjiang |
| Yarlungzangbo River | 1,787 (in Chinese territory) | 241,590 | Tibet (beyond the Chinese border it is the Bulama and Putela rivers) |
| Lancang River | 1,612 (in Chinese territory) | 153,960 (in Chinese territory) | Qinghai, Tibet, Yunnan (beyond the Chinese border it becomes the Meikong River) |
| Nujiang River | 1,540 (in Chinese territory) | 120,000 (in Chinese territory) | Tibet, Yunnan (beyond the Chinese border it is the Saerwen River) |
| Huaihe River | 1,000 | 187,000 | Henan, Anhui, Jiangsu |
| Wusuli River | 890 | 187,000 | Heilongjiang (the river forms the Sino-Soviet border) |
| Yalu River | 795 | 37,750 | Jilin, Liaoning (it forms the Sino-Korean border) |

River serves as the Sino-Soviet border. After passing beyond China's borders, the river flows towards the northeast, ultimately draining into the Pacific Ocean. It has a total length of 2,965 kilometers and a drainage area of 890,000 square kilometers inside China. Its main tributaries are the Jieya, the Songhua and the Wusuli rivers.

The Zhujiang River, the fourth longest in China, is the general name for three conjoining rivers: the Xijiang River, the Beijiang River and the Dongjiang River. The quantity of its discharge is second only to that of the Changjiang River. The Zhujiang River originates at Mount Maxiong in Zhanyi County, Yunnan Province, and from there traverses Yunnan, Guizhou, Guangxi, Guangdong, Hunan and Jiangxi, emptying into the South China Sea at Modaomen in Guangdong Province. It has a total length of 2,200 kilometers and a drainage area of 452,000 square kilometers.

The Grand Canal runs 1,794 kilometers from Beijing to Hangzhou, traversing Tianjin, Hebei, Shandong, Jiangsu and Zhejiang. Along the way it intersects the Haihe River, the Huanghe River, the Huaihe River, the Changjiang River and the Qiantang River.

The construction of the Grand Canal commenced in the 5th century B.C. (at the end of the Spring and Autumn period) and was completed after two large-scale expansions, the first carried out in the 7th century A.D. (Sui dynasty) and the second in the 13th century A.D. (Yuan dynasty). The Grand Canal was ancient China's greatest water conservancy project, and the services which it provides in irrigation, transportation and fresh-water aquiculture have benefited later generations down to the present day.

The Grand Canal

# CLIMATE

China may be divided into five major climatic zones — tropical, subtropical, warm-temperate, temperate, and frigid-temperate — which are much influenced by the monsoonal winds. Among these zones, the sub-tropical, warm-temperate and temperate zones occupy 70 percent of the country's territory.

Every winter from September and October through March and April, frigid winds sweep down across China from Mongolia and Siberia. As a result, northern Chinese winters are dry and cold, and the wintertime variation between northern and southern China is quite large — more than 30 degrees Centigrade in the case of Harbin and Guangzhou (see the accompanying chart). However, from April to September, due to the influence of the warm wet monsoon winds which blow inland from the Pacific and Indian oceans, the temperature variation between north and south is 4 degrees Centigrade.

The hottest area in China is the Turpan District in the Xinjiang Uygur Autonomous Region. Topographically, Xinjiang is the lowest point in China, with Aydingkol Lake at 154 meters below sea level. The average temperature in Turpan in July is 33 degrees Centigrade, while the average daytime temperature during the same month exceeds 40. The highest temperature ever recorded in this district was 47.6 (July 4, 1941).

China's coldest region is located in the Hailar District in the Hulun Beir League of Inner Mongolia, where the average temperature in January is −27.7 degrees Centigrade. Generally it does not go below −47.7 degrees Centigrade, though the lowest temperature ever recorded in this district was −51.5 (January 21, 1960).

In China, annual precipitation decreases gradually from the southeast to the northwest. In the humid southeast, precipitation averages 1,500 mm. annually, while in the arid northwest, the annual figure is 50 mm. Huoshaoliao in Taiwan Province has the heaviest precipitation in the country, with

The Scenic Jiuzhaigou in Sichuan

an average of 6,489 mm. per year, and once registered a record-breaking 8,408 mm.

Ruoqiang and Qiemo counties in the southern Xinjiang Uygur Autonomous Region are the most arid regions in the country, with an average annual precipitation of only 10 mm.

The distinct climatic features of each of China's regions can be roughly summarized as follows: Heilongjiang Province and northern Hulun Beir League of the Inner Mongolia Autonomous Region are entirely without summer. Hainan Island of Guangdong Province has a long summer and is virtually without winter. The Nansha Islands belonging to Guangdong Province are of the humid tropical monsoon climate. In the Huaihe River basin the four seasons are clearly differentiated. In the Kunming region of Yunnan Province the weather is spring-like all year round.

In the inland regions of the northwest, the summers are hot and winters cold. There is a considerable temperature variation between the daytime and night.

The western part of the Tibet-Qinghai Plateau is covered with snow throughout the year. It is a frigid region of high elevation.

The Subtropical Hainan Island

A Winter Scene in Harbin, a North China City

## COMPARATIVE CHART SHOWING THE AVERAGE TEMPERATURE IN 13 REGIONS OF CHINA IN JANUARY AND JULY
### (Centigrade)

|           | January  | July   |
|-----------|----------|--------|
| Harbin    | —19.7°   | 22.7°  |
| Beijing   | —4.7°    | 26.0°  |
| Xi'an     | —1.3°    | 26.7°  |
| Lanzhou   | —7.3°    | 22.4°  |
| Qingdao   | —2.6°    | 24.7°  |
| Turpan    | —9.5°    | 33.0°  |
| Shanghai  | 3.3°     | 27.9°  |
| Hangzhou  | 3.6°     | 28.7°  |
| Wuhan     | 2.8°     | 29.0°  |
| Chengdu   | 5.6°     | 25.8°  |
| Kunming   | 7.8°     | 19.9°  |
| Guilin    | 8.0°     | 28.3°  |
| Guangzhou | 13.4°    | 28.3°  |

# NATURE RESERVES

China now has 106 nature reserves which cover a total area of 3.9 million hectares. By the end of 1990, the number of reserves is planned to grow to 491, and occupy an area of 16.7 million hectares, or 1.74 percent of China's total land area. Of the present 106 reserves, three are part of the international Man and Biosphere Network; Wolong, Changbaishan and Dinghushan.

The Wolong reserve in Sichuan Province covers an area of 200,000 hectares, and is the home of 100 of China's 1,000 pandas and other rare species.

The Changbaishan reserve is the largest comprehensive wildlife reserve in China. It comprises 215,000 hectares in the northeastern province of Jilin.

The Dinghushan reserve in Guangdong Province is a sub tropical monsoon evergreen broadleaf forest zone which has preserved its primitive features almost intact. In this area of 270 hectares grow more than 2,000 higher plants.

Giant Panda

# RARE ANIMALS

China's nature reserves are the home of a number of rare species, such as panda, takin, golden monkey, gray golden monkey, white bear, hoary headed leaf monkey, macaque, gibbon, Manchurian tiger, Hainan mountain deer, Yangtze alligator and red-crowned crane. Other rare species found in China are David's deer, white-lipped deer, pangolin and lancelet, as well as the recently discovered crested ibis and Jiao Guai, previously thought extinct, and the white-finned dolphin, a species unique to China.

Golden Monkey

Takin

Jiao Guai

Manchurian Tiger

White-Finned Dolphin

Red-Crowned Crane

Crested Ibis

Macaque

## RARE PLANTS

Some of the rare plants to be found in China are the black spinulose fern, Chinese tulip tree, Chinese manglietiastum, pinus massioniana, gingko, dragon spruce, silver fir, giant sequoia, Chinese hemlock, dove tree, Korean pine, pseudotaxus chienii, pseudolarix ambilis, Parashorea chinencis, Chinese breschneidera, and Tukou cycas

Black Spinulose Tree Fern is an exquisite, ancient variety of high decorative value.

Cathaya Argyrophylla, or Silver Fir, is unique to China and the only member of its species and genus. It grows sparsely on some mountain ridges and rocky hill tops in a few scattered areas of Hunan, Sichuan, Guizhou and Guangxi.

Pseudotaxus Chienii is unique to China and is the only member of its species and genus now extant. With its snow-white fruit set off against its dark green leaves, it is strikingly beautiful.

Chinese Breschneidera is an ancient variety. It is unique to China and the only member of its species and genus now extant.

*Upper Left:*
A plant of the Tertiary Period, 7 to 65 million years ago, Pseudolarix Amabilis is unique to China and is one of the world famous ornamentals.

*Left:*
Unique to China, Tukou Cycas is found only in the two counties of Tukou and Ningnan in the Jinsha and Ganre river valleys, the northernmost latitude for the Cycas Family.

*Right:*
Discovered only recently, Parashorea Chinensis is unique to China and can be found only in one 20-square-kilometer area of Yunnan Province. It is a fine timber tree and can grow as high as 50 meters.

*Far Left:*
Davidia Involucrata, or Dove Tree, is a plant of the Tertiary Period and the only member of its species and genus now extant. Native to China, it has been introduced to many countries abroad and it is now a world famous decorative plant.

*Left:*
Chinese Manglietiastum, discovered quite recently, is the sole member of its species and genus.

*Lower Left:*
Ginkgo is a tree of ancient variety and very popular in China. It grows very slowly and can be as old as several thousand years.

*Below:*
Pinus Massoniana, found mainly in southwest China, is a plant of the Tertiary Period and it is the only member of its family now extant.

# CHINA'S POPULATION

China is a unified country comprising many different nationalities. Besides the majority Han, there are 55 other nationalities, including the Mongolian, Hui, Tibetan, Uygur, Miao, Yi, Zhuang, Bouyei, Korean, Manchu, Dong, Yao, Bai, Tujia and Hani.

According to the 1982 census, conducted on July 1, China has a total population of 1,031,882,511 persons. The population of the Han nationality in China's 29 provinces, municipalities and autonomous regions (not including Taiwan Province and Jinmen and Mazu Islands in Fujian Province) is 936,703,824, accounting for 93.3 percent of the total. The total population of all the other nationalities is 67,233,254, or 6.7 percent of the total. Each of the fifteen minority nationalities listed above has populations in excess of one million.

## HISTORY OF CHINA'S POPULATION CHANGE

| Year | Total Population |
|---|---|
| A.D.    2 (Western Han dynasty) | 59,590,000 |
| 755 (Tang dynasty) | 52,910,000 |
| 1080 (Song dynasty) | 33,300,000 |
| 1578 (Ming dynasty) | 60,960,000 |
| 1741 (Qing dynasty) | 143,410,000 |
| 1840 (Qing dynasty) | 412,000,000 |
| 1912 (Republic of China) | 405,810,000 |
| 1949 (Founding of People's Republic of China) | 541,670,000 |
| 1982 (July 1) | 1,031,882,511 |

## POPULATION AND AREA OF CHINA'S
## PROVINCES, MUNICIPALITIES AND AUTONOMOUS REGIONS

| Province, Municipality or Autonomous Region | Population | Area (km²) |
|---|---|---|
| Beijing Municipality | 9,230,687 | 16,807 |
| Tianjin Municipality | 7,764,141 | 11,305 |
| Hebei Province | 53,005,875 | 187,700 |
| Shanxi Province | 25,291,389 | 156,300 |
| Inner Mongolia Autonomous Region | 19,274,279 | 1,183,000 |
| Liaoning Province | 35,721,693 | 145,700 |
| Jilin Province | 22,560,053 | 180,000 |
| Heilongjiang Province | 32,665,546 | 469,000 |
| Shanghai Municipality | 11,859,748 | 6,185 |
| Jiangsu Province | 60,521,114 | 102,600 |
| Zhejiang Province | 38,884,603 | 102,000 |
| Anhui Province | 49,665,724 | 139,900 |
| Fujian Porvince | 25,931,106 | 120,000 |
| Jiangxi Province | 33,184,827 | 166,600 |
| Shandong Province | 74,419,054 | 153,300 |
| Henan Province | 74,422,739 | 167,000 |
| Hubei Province | 47,804,150 | 187,000 |
| Hunan Province | 54,008,851 | 210,000 |
| Guangdong Province | 59,299,220 | 212,000 |
| Guangxi Zhuang Autonomous Region | 36,420,960 | 236,200 |
| Sichuan Province | 99,713,310 | 570,000 |
| Guizhou Province | 28,552,997 | 176,300 |
| Yunnan Province | 32,553,817 | 394,000 |
| Tibet Autonomous Region | 1,892,393 | 1,228,400 |
| Shaanxi Province | 28,904,423 | 206,000 |
| Gansu Province | 19,569,261 | 454,000 |
| Qinghai Province | 3,895,706 | 721,500 |
| Ningxia Hui Autonomous Region | 3,895,578 | 60,000 |
| Xinjiang Uygur Autonomous Region | 13,081,681 | 1,600,000 |
| Taiwan Province | 18,270,749 | 35,989 |

# THE POPULATIONS OF CHINA'S NATIONALITIES
## (1982 CENSUS)

| | | | |
|---|---|---|---|
| Han | 936,703,824 | Xibe | 83,629 |
| Zhuang | 13,378,162 | Salar | 69,102 |
| Hui | 7,219,352 | Blang | 58,476 |
| Uygur | 5,957,112 | Gelo | 53,802 |
| Yi | 5,453,448 | Maonan | 38,135 |
| Miao | 5,030,897 | Tajik | 26,503 |
| Manchu | 4,299,159 | Pumi | 20,441 |
| Tibetan | 3,870,068 | Nu | 23,166 |
| Mongolian | 3,411,657 | Achang | 20,411 |
| Tujia | 2,832,743 | Ewenki | 19,343 |
| Bouyei | 2,120,469 | Ozbek | 12,453 |
| Korean | 1,763,870 | Benglong | 12,295 |
| Dong | 1,425,100 | Jing | 11,995 |
| Yao | 1,402,676 | Jino | 11,974 |
| Bai | 1,131,124 | Yugur | 10,569 |
| Hani | 1,058,836 | Bonan | 9,027 |
| Kazak | 907,582 | Moinba | 6,248 |
| Dai | 839,797 | Drung | 4,682 |
| Li | 817,562 | Oroqen | 4,132 |
| Lisu | 480,960 | Tatar | 4,127 |
| She | 368,832 | Russian | 2,935 |
| Lahu | 304,174 | Luoba | 2,065 |
| Va | 298,591 | Gaoshan | 1,549 |
| Shui | 286,487 | Hezhen | 1,476 |
| Dongxiang | 279,397 | | |
| Naxi | 245,154 | Other unclassifi- | |
| Tu | 159,426 | ed nationalities | 879,201 |
| Kirgiz | 113,999 | | |
| Qiang | 102,768 | Foreign nationals | |
| Daur | 94,014 | who have be- | |
| Jingpo | 93,008 | come Chinese | |
| Mulam | 90,426 | citizens | 4,842 |

## RATE OF INCREASE OF CHINA'S POPULATION
### (1949-1981)

| Year | Population Size (in thousands) | Rate of Natural Increase (per thousand) |
|------|-------------------------------|------------------------------------------|
| 1949 | 541,670 | 16.0 |
| 1952 | 574,820 | 20.0 |
| 1957 | 646,530 | 23.2 |
| 1965 | 725,380 | 28.5 |
| 1978 | 958,090 | 12.05 |
| 1980 | 982,550 | 12.0 |
| 1981 | 996,220 | 14.55 |

Health Specialists Giving Advice on Family Planning

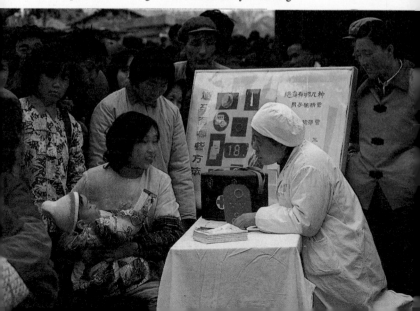

# CHINA'S PROJECTED POPULATION INCREASE IN NEXT 50 YEARS IF EACH WOMAN BEARS ONE CHILD

| Year | Population Size (100 millions) | Number of Women of Childbearing Age (100 millions) | Births (millions) | Deaths (millions) | Rate of Natural Increase (per thousand) | Able-bodied Workers (100 millions) | Elderly (millions) | Average Age of Entire Population | Number of Dependants (per person) |
|---|---|---|---|---|---|---|---|---|---|
| 1980 | 9.78 | 2.07 | 16.50 | 7.35 | 9.50 | 5.2 | 49.6 | 26.8 | 0.89 |
| 1985 | 10.02 | 2.43 | 11.40 | 7.87 | 3.50 | 6.1 | 58.2 | 29.1 | 0.67 |
| 1990 | 10.21 | 2.79 | 10.20 | 7.00 | 3.02 | 6.9 | 67.6 | 31.7 | 0.48 |
| 1995 | 10.37 | 2.99 | 11.30 | 8.15 | 2.95 | 7.4 | 79.4 | 33.8 | 0.40 |
| 2000 | 10.50 | 3.00 | 10.80 | 8.92 | 1.87 | 7.6 | 93.6 | 35.9 | 0.38 |
| 2005 | 10.54 | 2.80 | 9.10 | 9.51 | −0.39 | 7.5 | 108.0 | 38.0 | 0.40 |
| 2010 | 10.45 | 2.65 | 7.00 | 9.73 | −2.63 | 7.4 | 123.3 | 40.5 | 0.42 |
| 2015 | 10.26 | 2.36 | 5.56 | 9.73 | −4.06 | 7.1 | 149.7 | 43.2 | 0.44 |
| 2020 | 10.03 | 2.00 | 5.19 | 9.82 | −4.64 | 6.8 | 190.6 | 45.7 | 0.48 |
| 2025 | 9.78 | 1.65 | 4.95 | 10.25 | −5.21 | 6.3 | 220.7 | 48.5 | 0.56 |
| 2030 | 9.51 | 1.43 | 4.53 | 10.11 | −5.87 | 5.5 | 280.8 | 51.0 | 0.72 |

A Poster Advocating Family Planning

## CHINA'S PROJECTED POPULATION GROWTH IN NEXT 100 YEARS

(100 millions)

| Year | Average Number of Births per Woman | | | | | |
|------|------|------|------|------|------|------|
| | 1.0 | 1.5 | 2.0 | 2.3 (1978 average) | 2.5 | 3.0 (1975 average) |
| 1980 | 9.78 | 9.78 | 9.78 | 9.80 | 9.83 | 9.85 |
| 1990 | 10.21 | 10.43 | 10.83 | 11.15 | 11.36 | 11.75 |
| 2000 | 10.50 | 11.25 | 12.17 | 12.82 | 13.23 | 14.15 |
| 2010 | 10.45 | 11.62 | 13.04 | 14.07 | 14.72 | 16.28 |
| 2020 | 10.03 | 11.69 | 13.79 | 15.38 | 16.41 | 19.02 |
| 2030 | 9.51 | 11.71 | 14.60 | 16.81 | 18.28 | 22.19 |
| 2040 | 8.79 | 11.49 | 15.09 | 17.97 | 19.95 | 25.43 |
| 2050 | 7.71 | 10.82 | 15.32 | 19.03 | 21.64 | 29.23 |
| 2060 | 6.13 | 9.67 | 15.07 | 19.68 | 23.00 | 33.09 |
| 2070 | 4.58 | 8.49 | 14.78 | 20.36 | 24.48 | 37.57 |
| 2080 | 3.70 | 7.77 | 14.72 | 21.19 | 26.24 | 42.64 |

# FAMILY PLANNING

China has the world's largest population and thus China's ability to control its population growth is a matter of concern for the entire world.

Qian Xinzhong, Chairman of China's Family Planning Commission, won the 1983 United Nations Population Award for his work in organizing and directing research in China's family planning program and contraceptives. This is a recognition of the great importance which has been attached to family planning work in the People's Republic of China since its founding in 1949.

In 1953, the Government Administrative Council entrusted the Ministry of Health with the responsibility of carrying out family planning work and issued a handbook entitled *Methods of Birth Control and Abortion*, as well as other reading matters designed to disseminate knowledge about birth control. The issuance of these publications was accompanied by an extensive educational campaign among the masses.

In June 1957, during the Fourth Session of the First People's Congress, the eminent Chinese economist Ma Yinchu (1882-1982) first introduced his "New Population Theory" in which he advocated controlling the growth of China's population and promoted eugenics.

In 1962, the Chinese government stressed the policy that family planning is fundamental to China's socialist construction. In 1963, research was conducted on oral contraceptives wherein these drugs were used on a trial basis in clinical practice. In 1964, the Central Government established an Office of Family Planning, and work in this field began to be carried out in progressive stages, beginning in the most densely populated urban areas.

In 1979, the Third Plenum of the Eleventh Party Central Committee announced that in 1980, China's annual rate of population increase declined to below ten per thousand. On September 25, 1980, the Central Committee of the Chinese Communist Party issued an open letter to all members of the Chinese Communist Party and Chinese Communist Youth

League calling on them to take the lead in implementing the Party's family planning policy by having only one child per couple.

In June 1980, China established the Family Planning Association. Since its establishment, this association has actively cooperated with the World Family Planning Organization and has participated in a variety of international exchanges.

In 1982, China's fourth Constitution was adopted and promulgated. Article 25 of the Constitution stipulates: "The nation pursues a policy of family planning in order to adapt the pace of population increase to the nation's social and economic development." In September of the same year, the political report of the 12th Party Congress pointed out: "The population problem is of crucial importance to our country's economic and social development. Practicing family planning is one of our basic national policies. By the end of the 20th century, we must work hard to contain our country's population within the limit of one billion and two hundred million people."

To promote family planning, the Chinese government provides all married citizens with free contraceptives and offers single-child families certain material incentives and rewards, such as giving only-children priority in entering kindergartens and primary schools. In addition, the heads of single-child households are given a monthly living subsidy apart from their salaries.

Since its inception in China, the family planning movement has already produced positive results. The natural rate of population increase, which in 1952 rose to nearly 20 per thousand per annum, dropped to 14.5 per thousand in 1981. That is to say, if China's population had continued to increase at the 1952 annual rate of 20 per thousand, during the nine-year period between 1971 and 1979, China's population would have increased by an additional 56 million; in the year 1979 alone, this would have amounted to 10 million more births than those which actually occurred.

Judging from the vigorous manner in which China is pursuing its birth control campaign, as long as the government and people continue to make concerted efforts in this direction, the future prospects of China's controlling the growth of its enormous population will be bright.

# MINORITY NATIONALITIES AND ETHNIC WORK

Besides the Han nationality which makes up the majority of the country's population, the combined total of her 55 known minority nationalities is 6.7 million, or 6.7 percent of the national total according to the 1982 census. Small as their population is, they live widely scattered across the country.

The minority autonomous areas, where most of these people live, cover 62 percent of the country's total land area.

## LOCATION

China's minority people in general live in highlands or hilly pastoral or forest regions

that are mostly situated in the frontier areas. However, historical events, like repeated migrations, sizable reclamation projects, forced migrations into frontier regions and changes of feudal dynasties, have combined to bring about the present situation in which the various minorities live both together in mixed groups as well as in their own compact communities. In the Xinjiang Uygur Autonomous Region, for instance, apart from the Uygurs, there are a dozen other nationalities also resident. To cite another example, Yunnan Province is home for as many as 22 minorities.

Due to historical reasons, there are certain ethnically variegated regions where different nationalities have been dwelling together not in mixed communities but rather in a ladder-like distribution arrangement. In Yunnan and Guizhou provinces as well as in the Guangxi Zhuang Autonomous Region, for example, the Hans generally live in cities and towns, the Zhuang, Bouyei, Dai and Bai nationalities live on plains, while the other minorities reside on hillsides at different levels. In Xishuangbanna, a subtropical region in southwest China, most of the 210,000 Dais for the most part inhabit the plain areas while the other minority peoples, a group totalling more than 200,000 people which includes the Hani, Blang, Jino, Lahu, Miao, Yao and Va, live in the hills.

Minority peoples such as the Tibetans, Manchus and Huis live in concentrated communities in one or several regions, while part of their members are scattered in other parts of the country intermingling with the Hans and other nationalities.

## POPULATION

Before 1949, owing to the oppressive policies pursued by the Kuomintang and the feudal social systems which existed within the minority areas themselves, most of the minority people lived in dire poverty and lacked medical care. The resultant high infant mortality rate and short average life span led to a very low rate of population growth. Since the founding of the People's Republic in 1949, the People's Government has appropriated large amounts of manpower, materials and funds to promote economic development in the minority areas. This has greatly improved the living standards and health services there. Furthermore, in carrying out the family planning program, the state, while advocating that the Han people have only one child per couple, has given preferential treatment to the minority people. National autonomous areas are permitted to work out their own family planning policies, taking into account such factors as population density and growth.

The number of minority nationalities whose population has surpassed the million mark has increased from 10 in 1964 to 15 at present. Some minorities have more than doubled the size of their population over the past 30 years. The population of Mongolians, for instance, has grown to over 3.4 million as against 830,000 on the eve of liberation. Similarly the Hezhens have increased from some 300 to over 1,400 and the Jinos from 4,000 to 12,000 over the same period.

## EQUALITY OF NATIONALITIES

China's ethnic work is aimed at promoting equality, unity and mutual assistance among all its nationalities, strengthening their solidarity and developing their economies. The spirit of treating the nation's different ethnic groups equally has been written into all versions of the Chinese Constitution, each of which stipulates: "It is the duty of citizens of the People's Republic of China to safeguard the unity of the country and the unity of all its nationalities.

"All nationalities in the People's Republic of China are equal. The state protects the lawful rights and interests of the minority nationalities and upholds and develops the relationship of equality, unity and mutual assistance among all of China's nationalities. Discrimination against and oppression of any nationality is prohibited; and any acts which undermine the unity of the nationalities or instigate their secession are prohibited."

In order to implement effectively the above ethnic policies, various organizations have been set up at different levels throughout the country. Under the National People's Congress, the supreme organ of state power, there is the Nationalities' Committee. It is responsible for working out enactments concerning the state's handling of ethnic problems as well as submitting autonomy regulations and specific regulations put forward by the autonomous areas to the National People's Congress and its Standing Committee for their approval. Beneath the State Council, the highest administrative organ of the state, there is the State Nationalities' Affairs Commission. Some other departments under the State Council such as the ministries of commerce, culture, education and public health, also have their own organizations in charge of ethnic work. Within the National Committee of the Chinese People's Political Consultative Conference, there is also a section with the task of investigating the implementation of ethnic policies and determining their effectiveness.

At the local level, the people's congresses of some provinces and autonomous regions have a nationalities' committee or section. The governments of many provinces, autonomous regions and major cities include a nationalities' affairs committee or section. Several provincial governments also include separate nationalities' religious affairs offices. Below the provincial and autonomous region levels, the governments of quite a number of prefectures, municipalities and counties also include nationalities' committees or sections or religious affairs offices. In other places, full-time personnel are appointed to take charge of ethnic work in the areas where there are scattered minority groups.

As early as 1949, the Central People's Government already began to take steps to eliminate the historical inequalities which still existed between the nationalities. New China's earliest provisional Constitution, the Common Program of the Chinese People's Political Consultative Conference, expressly provided for the equality of all nationalities, thus combating Han chauvinism. Then in 1951, the Central People's Government, acting on the spirit of the Common Program, issued a directive to do away with terms of address, place names, inscriptions on stone tablets and scrolls which were demeaning to ethnic minorities. In 1952, the Central People's Government issued a program for national autonomy which established the legal framework for China's autonomous areas and promulgated laws safeguarding the rights of members of minority groups resident outside of these areas. The same provisions have been included in all later versions of the Chinese Constitution.

Each of the 56 nationalities is represented at the National People's Congress. Even the smallest nationality, the Hezhen, has a deputy attending the congress. The proportion of minority deputies in the total number of deputies exceeds that of the minority population in the country's total (10.9 percent at the present congress).

## MINORITY CADRES

Minority cadres are to be found among government leaders at all levels, from the central to the local. As minority cadres are familiar with the history, customs, thinking and sentiments of their own people, fluent in their own native languages, and possess detailed knowledge of concrete conditions of their localities, the training of minority cadres is an effective guarantee to ensure their constitutional rights and their right to manage their own affairs.

The Chinese Communist Party has always attached great importance to training minority cadres. As early as the period of the War of Resistance Against Japan (1937-1945), an institute for training minority cadres was founded in the capital of the liberated areas at Yan'an — the first such institute in China. In 1950, immediately after the founding of the People's Republic, the Central Institute for Nationalities was set up in Beijing to train minority cadres. And in order to meet the growing demand for minority cadres necessitated by national reconstruction, regional autonomy, and the im-

plementation of ethnic policies, nine other similar institutes were set up. They are the Northwest Institute in Lanzhou, Gansu Province; the Southwest Institute in Chengdu, Sichuan Province; the South-Central Institute in Wuchang, Hubei Province; the Guangdong Institute in Guangzhou; the Guangxi Institute in Nanning; the Yunnan Institute in Kunming; the Guizhou Institute in Guiyang; the Qinghai Institute in Xining, and the Tibet Institute in Xianyang, Shaanxi Province. Furthermore, eight universities and two colleges also conduct special classes for minority people.

These government efforts have sizably increased the number of minority cadres. Statistics compiled at the end of 1981 show that minority cadres totaled 1.02 million, or 5.4 percent of all the cadres in the country. Meanwhile the number of minority cadres in leading posts has also increased. The leading officials in the five autonomous regions, 30 autonomous prefectures and the large majority of other organs of self-government in the country were, and still are, minority people. The percentage of specialized minority personnel working in the minority areas had grown from some 10 percent in the fifties to 30 percent by the end of 1981.

## MINORITY LANGUAGES

All of China's minority nationalities have their own languages with the exception of the Huis and the Manchus who use the Han language. The 50-odd minority nationalities speak a total of more than 60 languages, as certain minorities use more than one language.

Most of the 60-odd languages belong to the Sino-Tibetan and the Altaic families, a minority belonging to the South Asian, the Austronesian and the Indo-European families.

It is the policy of the Chinese government to respect and pro-

## THE WORLD'S LONGEST EPIC

With more than a million lines, the Tibetan folk epic *Gesar* (*The Deeds of King Gesar, the Destroyer of Enemies*) is the longest epic in the world. For the past thousand years it has been spread both orally and in the form of handwritten manuscripts in the Tibetan and Mongolian inhabited regions of Tibet, Sichuan, Gansu, Yunnan and Inner Mongolia. In its full length, the narrative poem comprises 30 chapters which are not only of literary value but are also of academic interest to researchers in the fields of ethnology, theology and history, as they constitute virtually an encyclopedia of ancient Tibetan society.

*Gesar* is a narrative of the life of an 11th century chieftain of the Lingduo tribe, an ethnic group which in ancient times inhabited the region near the source of the Huanghe River in Qinghai and the upper reaches of the Yalong River in Sichuan. A master of martial arts and a brilliant military commander, Gesar cut a heroic figure and was loved and esteemed by his people. This extended narrative poem based on his life was not written all at once but was gradually created over a long period of time in the process of repeated re-tellings.

Over the course of the years *Gesar* was transmitted from Tibet to Mongolia, Central Asia, Turkey, Sikkim and Bhutan. Abridged translations of the epic have also been published in English, French, German, Russian, Indian, Mongolian and Latin.

Celebrating the 30th Anniversary of the Founding of the Aba Tibetan Autonomous Prefecture

tect the freedom of all minorities to use and develop their own languages, spoken or written; assist those minorities who have no written script in working out one or adopting a suitable one; and to assist those minorities whose written languages are imperfect in improving or reforming them.

In line with this policy, the organs of self-government employ the spoken and written language in common use in the locality in performing their functions. The Central Government lends support to the minority people's cultural and educational undertakings using their own languages and encourages the Han personnel working in the minority areas to study the languages of the local minority people. Furthermore, the Chinese government has helped nine minorities devise a total of 13 written languages based on the Latin alphabet. These peoples are the Zhuang, Bouyei, Miao, Li, Naxi, Lisu, Hani, Va and Dong. It has also helped five minorities reform or improve their written languages, namely the Uygur, Kazak, Dai, Jingpo and Lahu. As a result, more than 30 minorities now have their own written languages, as compared to 20 before 1949.

The policy for ensuring equality in the use of languages for the minorities has been given legal form in the Chinese Constitution, the Program for the Implementation of Regional National Autonomy and China's Law of Criminal Procedure. The sixth article of China's Law of Criminal Procedure reads: "Citizens of all nationalities have the right of using their own languages in criminal proceedings. The people's court, the people's procuratorate and the public security organ shall provide interpretation for a litigant participant unacquainted with the spoken and written language commonly used in the locality.

"In districts compactly inhabited by a minority nationality or by a number of nationalities, trials and inquiries shall be conducted in the commonly used spoken language in the locality, written judgments, public notices, and other documents issued in the commonly used written language in the locality."

In fact, schooling in the primary and middle schools or colleges, if any, in the areas inhabited by Mongolians, Tibetans, Uygurs, Kazaks and Koreans is entirely or partially conducted in their respective languages. The primary schools (or at least their junior classes) in the areas peopled by Xibes, Dais, Jingpos, Yis, Zhuangs, Lisus, Lahus, Vas or Kirgizes are taught in their respective languages. Some minority groups, while themselves using textbooks written in Han or the languages of other minorities, use their own languages as supplementary means of teaching.

Mongolian, Tibetan, Uygur, Kazak, Korean and Dai are used officially by the Party and government organizations in the relevant autonomous areas. In other areas, the autonomous organs employ the spoken and written language or languages in common use in the locality in their newspapers, directives and documents. The inscriptions on the official seals and signboards of organizations, factories and schools, coupons and certificates issued by the local governments are also in their respective local languages.

The Central People's Broadcasting Station regularly presents programs in Mongolian, Tibetan, Uygur, Kazak and Korean. All the successive National People's Congresses have issued their documents in Mongolian, Tibetan and Uygur as well as the Han language. Simultaneous interpretation is provided for the Mongolian, Tibetan, Uygur and Yi deputies.

## MINORITY ECONOMIES

Economically, the minority areas are generally backward compared with the Han areas. For this there are many historical reasons. In pre-1949 China, the nationality minority peoples were oppressed by a cruel feudal system which reduced them to the status of slaves or serfs of the landowners of their own nationality, while at the same time they were badly discriminated against by the Han-dominated national regimes. All this meant that their productive forces never advanced beyond a rudimentary stage of development.

After the founding of New China, the People's Government simultaneously carried out democratic reforms and socialist transformation in the minority areas. As a result, the earlier system of exploitation, oppression and discrimination was done away with, unleashing productive forces held back throughout the ages.

After reforming the social systems of the minority nationalities, the People's Government shifted its attention to helping them with economic construction. The successful result thus obtained is impressive: the gross output value of agricultural and industrial production in the minority areas in 1980 was 8.56 times greater than that in 1949, representing an average annual increase of 7.6 percent. This was accompanied by a marked improvement in the people's living standards.

In helping the minority areas, the state has adopted the following measures:

1. To adopt a flexible approach. That is to say, to work out policies, systems, measures of production management in strict accordance with the people's national characteristics, the local conditions and the people's aspirations. It is also meant to maintain all those current policies, regulations and measures that raise production and improve the people's living standards while revising or discarding those that fetter the productive forces.

2. Increasing the people's income while easing their economic burdens. This is done by raising the state purchasing prices for agricultural produce, livestock and animal products; reducing or eliminating agricultural, stockbreeding, trade or commercial taxes; and reducing the quotas of grain and animal products that the producers are required to sell to the state. In

Tibet, for instance, the local government in 1980 suspended the taxation of agricultural and stockbreeding taxes and taxation of collective enterprises, individual craftsmen and traders. In 1982, before the period of suspension ended, it was extended for three more years, and in Ngari Prefecture for even four years.

3. Helping the minority areas map out guidelines for economic development, which are based on detailed surveys of the natural resources within each area.

4. To encourage improvement in the system of production. The Central Government is making efforts to popularize the contract responsibility system in the minority areas. This system includes two alternative forms: the first is to divide up the work among the households of a certain village and assign appropriate production quotas to each; the second is to fix an output quota for each production team. In either case, each individual's income is determined by his output. This system has yielded positive economic results, as it provides tremendous impetus to the producers' enthusiasm for work.

5. To give substantial financial assistance in boosting economic construction and production. Despite its recent financial

A Miao Girl in Her National Costume

difficulties the state annually allocates special subsidies totaling over one billion yuan (about 500 million U.S. dollars) to the minority areas primarily for economic construction. Furthermore, the government appropriated an additional sum of 40 to 50 million yuan (about 20 to 25 million U.S. dollars) and supplied certain gold, silver, timber and other materials for use in producing goods needed specially by the minorities, such as ornaments, which constitute part of their traditional costume.

6. To encourage technical and economic cooperation between the minority areas and the more developed areas. The minority areas have rich natural resources but are lacking in technical expertise and funds. Thus the Central Government has called upon the Han areas to give technical and financial aid to the minority areas in developing their natural resources. In response to this call, Beijing has been supplying assistance to Inner Mongolia, Hebei to Guizhou, Jiangsu to Guangxi and Xinjiang, Shandong to Qinghai, Tianjin to Gansu, and Shanghai to Yunnan and Ningxia. Projects of this type launched from 1980 to 1982 period number 1,178. So far, one-third of them have been carried through to completion.

These efforts have brought about positive results in the minority areas. In 1981, the gross value of farm production in the autonomous areas was up 312 percent from the 1949 figure. In the intervening 32 years, grain output has risen by 191 percent and cotton output has increased more than ten times. Production of oil-bearing seeds, tobacco, tea, sub-tropical economic crops and medicinal herbs has also registered impressive growth.

Meanwhile, the livestock total has reached 117 million head by the end of 1981, 30 percent of the national total and more than four times as many as that registered in these areas at the end of 1949.

Even more impressive progress has been attained in industry, trade and transport and communications. The gross value of their industrial output in the minority areas in 1981 was 44 times the figure of 1949, representing an annual rise of 12.7 percent over a period of 30 years. Railway links have been established between four of the five autonomous regions and other parts of the country while a railway is under construction leading to Tibet, known as the "roof of the world". As of 1981 the mileage of railway in operation in the autonomous areas was 3.5 times the figure of 1949. The pace of highway construction has been even faster, 18 times the 1949 figure. In terms of trade, the gross value of commodities which the minority areas buy from the Han areas has gone up 30 times and the total retail sales of commodities within the minority areas have increased nearly 22 times. The Chinese minority areas are witnessing the beginning of a period of unprecedented prosperity.

# ADMINISTRATIVE DIVISIONS

China is divided into 30 administrative areas, each with the status comparable to that of a state in the United States. They are the three municipalities directly under the Central Government, namely, Beijing, Tianjin and Shanghai; the 22 provinces and the five autonomous regions.

Each of the administrative areas is subdivided into cities under the provincial government, districts and autonomous prefectures. These are then further subdivided into cities under the district or autonomous prefecture governments, counties, autonomous counties and towns. The lowest administrative units are urban neighborhoods, townships, nationality townships and country villages. Their respective administrative organs are residents' committees, township people's governments and villagers' committees. The townships and villages come under the leadership of the county they are in or else of a city which has the equivalent status of a county. The townships and villages attached to cities under the provincial government are under the leadership of the city's districts. People's communes, production brigades and production teams were formerly in charge of both administrative and production affairs, but are now only in charge of the latter. The township people's governments and villagers' committees manage local public and administrative affairs such as public welfare, mediation of villagers' disputes, and public security. In the self-governing minority areas, the township people's governments and villagers' committees perform a similar administrative function.

As China is still carrying out administrative readjustment and reform, the future may bring changes in China's administrative structure, such as the establishment of additional special economic zones.

# ADMINISTRATIVE DIVISIONS OF THE PEOPLE'S REPUBLIC OF CHINA

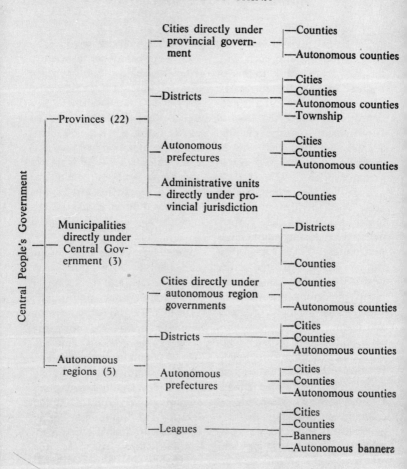

# CHINA'S PROVINCES AND AUTONOMOUS REGIONS AND THEIR CAPITALS

| Provinces and Autonomous Regions | Provincial Capitals |
| --- | --- |
| Hebei Province | Shijiazhuang |
| Shanxi Province | Taiyuan |
| Inner Mongolia Autonomous Region | Hohhot |
| Liaoning Province | Shenyang |
| Jilin Province | Changchun |
| Heilongjiang Province | Harbin |
| Jiangsu Province | Nanjing |
| Zhejiang Province | Hangzhou |
| Anhui Province | Hefei |
| Fujian Province | Fuzhou |
| Jiangxi Province | Nanchang |
| Shandong Province | Jinan |
| Henan Province | Zhengzhou |
| Hubei Province | Wuhan |
| Hunan Province | Changsha |
| Guangdong Province | Guangzhou |
| Guangxi Zhuang Autonomous Region | Nanning |
| Sichuan Province | Chengdu |
| Guizhou Province | Guiyang |
| Yunnan Province | Kunming |
| Tibet Autonomous Region | Lhasa |
| Shaanxi Province | Xi'an |
| Gansu Province | Lanzhou |
| Qinghai Province | Xining |
| Ningxia Hui Autonomous Region | Yinchuan |
| Xinjiang Uygur Autonomous Region | Urumqi |
| Taiwan Province | Taibei |

# ORGANS OF STATE POWER

The National People's Congress is the highest organ of state power. It is composed of deputies elected by the provinces, autonomous regions and municipalities directly under the Central Government, and by the armed forces. It is elected for a term of five years. Its permanent body is the Standing Committee of the National People's Congress. The National People's Congress exercises the following functions and powers:

(1) to amend the Constitution;

(2) to supervise the enforcement of the Constitution;

(3) to enact and amend basic statutes concerning criminal offences, civil affairs, the state organs and other matters;

(4) to elect the President and the Vice-President of the People's Republic of China;

(5) to decide on the choice of the Premier of the State Council upon nomination by the President of the People's Republic of China, and to decide on the choice of the Vice-Premiers, State Councilors, Ministers in charge of ministries or commissions and the Auditor-General and the Secretary-General of the State Council upon nomination by the Premier;

(6) to elect the Chairman of the Central Military Commission and, upon nomination by the Chairman, to decide on the choice of others on the Central Military Commission;

(7) to elect the President of the Supreme People's Court;

(8) to elect the Procurator-General of the Supreme People's Procuratorate;

(9) to examine and approve the plan for national economic and social development and the report on its implementation;

(10) to examine and approve the state budget and the report on its implementation;

(11) to alter or annul inappropriate decisions of the Standing Committee of the National People's Congress;

(12) to approve the establishment of provinces, autonomous regions, and municipalities directly under the Central Government;

(13) to decide on the establishment of special administrative regions and the systems to be instituted there;

(14) to decide on questions of war and peace; and

(15) to exercise such other functions and powers as the highest organ of state power should exercise.

The National People's Congress has the power to recall:

(1) the President and the Vice-President of the People's Republic of China;

(2) the Premier, Vice-Premiers, State Councilors, Ministers in charge of ministries or commissions and the Auditor-General and the Secretary-General of the State Council;

(3) the Chairman of the Central Military Commission and others on the commission;

(4) the President of the Supreme People's Court; and

(5) the Procurator-General of the Supreme People's Procuratorate.

The National People's Congress elects, and has the power to recall, all those on its Standing Committee.

No one on the Standing Committee of the National People's Congress shall hold any post in any of the administrative, judicial or procuratorial organs of the state.

The State Council, that is, the Central People's Government, of the People's Republic of China is the executive body of the highest organ of state power; it is the highest organ of state administration.

The State Council exercises the following functions and powers:

(1) to adopt administrative measures, enact administrative rules and regulations and issue decisions and orders in accordance with the Constitution and the statutes;

(2) to submit proposals to the National People's Congress or its Standing Committee;

(3) to lay down the tasks and responsibilities of the ministries and commissions of the State Council, to exercise unified leadership over the work of the ministries and commissions and to direct all other administrative work of a national character that does not fall within the jurisdiction of the ministries and commissions;

(4) to exercise unified leadership over the work of local organs of state administration at different levels throughout the country, and to lay down the detailed division of functions and powers between the Central Government and the organs of state administration of provinces, autonomous regions and municipalities directly under the Central Government;

(5) to draw up and implement the plan for national economic and social development and the state budget;

(6) to direct and administer economic affairs and urban and rural development;

(7) to direct and administer affairs of education, science, culture, public health, physical culture and family planning;

(8) to direct and administer civil affairs, public security, judicial administration, supervision and other related matters;

(9) to conduct foreign affairs and conclude treaties and agreements with foreign states;

(10) to direct and administer the building of national defense;

(11) to direct and administer affairs concerning the nationalities, and to safeguard the equal rights of minority nationalities and the right of autonomy of the national autonomous areas;

(12) to protect the legitimate rights and interests of Chinese nationals residing abroad and protect the lawful rights and interests of returned overseas Chinese and of the family members of Chinese nationals residing abroad;

(13) to alter or annul inappropriate orders, directives and regulations issued by the ministries or commissions;

(14) to approve the geographic division of provinces, autonomous regions and municipalities directly under the Central Government, and to approve the establishment and geographic division of autonomous prefectures, counties, autonomous counties and cities;

(15) to decide on the enforcement of martial law in parts of provinces, autonomous regions and municipalities directly under the Central Government;

(16) to examine and decide on the size of administrative organs and, in accordance with the law, to appoint, remove and train administrative officers, appraise their work and reward or punish them; and

(17) to exercise such other functions and powers as the National People's Congress or its Standing Committee may assign it.

The Supreme People's Court is the highest judicial organ. All cases handled by the people's courts, except for those involving special circumstances as specified by law, shall be heard in public. The accused has the right of defense. The people's courts shall, in accordance with the law, exercise judicial power independently and are not subject to interference by administrative organs, public organizations or individuals. The people's procuratorates of the People's Republic of China are state organs for legal supervision.

People's procuratorates shall, in accordance with the law, exercise procuratorial power independently and are not subject to interference by administrative organs, public organizations or individuals.

The Ancient Armillary Sphere

## THE WORLD'S FIRST ASTRONOMICAL CLOCK

One of the most outstanding achievements of ancient Chinese astronomy was the invention of numerous different astronomical instruments, such as the armillary sphere (an astronomical model with solid rings, all circles of a single sphere, used to display relationships among the principal celestial bodies).

During the Eastern Han dynasty (25-220 A.D.), the astronomer Zhang Heng invented a device which combined the functions of a water clock and armillary sphere. It used a gear wheel system to link the armillary sphere with the water clock, the motive power of water dripping through the clock being used to rotate the rings of the armillary sphere at a steady pace.

Slightly over 800 years later this device was further improved upon by the Northern Song scientist Su Song, who supervised the construction of a 12-meter-high observatory instrument which functioned simultaneously as an armillary sphere, water clock and astroscope and could be used to follow the movements of celestial bodies from east to west. The water clock was powered by the constant flow of water used to rotate its gear wheels at intervals. Its time-keeping mechanism was of a particularly ingenious construction, making use of an escape device which many scientists now believe was the direct forerunner of the escape wheel used in modern clocks today.

# A LIST OF THE CHAIRMEN AND VICE-CHAIRMEN OF THE SUCCESSIVE NATIONAL PEOPLE'S CONGRESSES

The First NPC:
Chairman: Liu Shaoqi
Vice-Chairmen:

Soong Ching Ling, Lin Boqu, Li Jishen, Zhang Lan, Luo Ronghuan, Shen Junru, Guo Moruo, Huang Yanpei, Peng Zhen, Li Weihan, Chen Shutong, Dalai Bstan-dzin Rgyamtsho, Saifudin

General Secretary: Peng Zhen

The Second NPC:
Chairman: Zhu De
Vice-Chairmen:

Lin Boqu, Li Jishen, Luo Ronghuan, Shen Junru, Guo Moruo, Huang Yanpei, Peng Zhen, Li Weihan, Chen Shutong, Dalai Bstan-dzin Rgyamtsho, Saifudin, Cheng Qian, Panchen Erdeni, He Xiangning, Liu Bocheng, Lin Feng

General Secretary: Peng Zhen

The Third NPC:
Chairman: Zhu De
Vice-Chairmen:

Peng Zhen, Liu Bocheng, Li Jingquan, Kang Sheng, Guo Moruo, He Xiangning, Huang Yanpei, Chen Shutong, Li Xuefeng, Xu Xiangqian, Yang Mingxuan, Cheng Qian, Saifudin, Lin Feng, Liu Ningyi, Zhang Zhizhong, Ngapoi Ngawang Jigme, Zhou Jianren

General Secretary: Liu Ningyi

The Fourth NPC:
Chairman: Zhu De
Vice-Chairmen:

Dong Biwu, Soong Ching Ling, Kang Sheng, Liu Bocheng, Wu De, Wei Guoqing, Saifudin, Guo Moruo, Xu Xiangqian, Nie Rongzhen, Chen Yun, Tan Zhenlin, Li Jingquan, Zhang Bingcheng, Cai Chang, Ulanhu, Ngapoi Ngawang Jigme, Zhou Jianren, Xu Deheng, Hu Juewen, Li Suwen, Yao Lianwei

General Secretary: Ji Pengfei

The Fifth NPC:
Chairman: Ye Jianying

# THE INVENTION OF THE COMPASS

The invention of the compass in ancient China did much
to speed the development of navigation. More than 2,000
years ago it was discovered in China that when natural
magnetite was ground into the shape of a spoon and then
spun upon a dish it would come to rest with its handle
pointing southwards. This device is mentioned in the works
of Han Fei, a Chinese philosopher of the third century B.C.,
and its use and development are expounded in considerable
detail in *Mengxi's Notes,* a collection of essays authored by
Chen Kuo in the Northern Song dynasty (960-1127).

In the 11th century A.D., the Chinese made a significant
improvement over the earliest, primitive compass. They
rubbed a steel needle against natural magnetite, causing it
to become magnetized in the process. This magnetized
needle was then hung or allowed to float in a cup of water,
where it would invariably point due south. Later, this
device was further refined by fitting it with a dish, forming
the prototype of the modern compass.

China was the first country to use the compass. The device
did not make its appearance in the rest of the civilized world
until the beginning of the 13th century.

# THE CHINESE PEOPLE'S POLITICAL CONSULTATIVE CONFERENCE

During the prolonged period of the Chinese people's revolutionary struggle, a broad united democratic front organization was established under the leadership of the Chinese Communist Party. This organization, the Chinese People's Political Consultative Conference (CPPCC), seeks to unite China's democratic parties and personages, mass organizations, minority nationality personages, patriots from various intellectual circles, socialist laborers, as well as patriots from Taiwan, Hongkong, Macao and overseas Chinese. The CPPCC is a consultative and advisory organ. It consists of delegates representing the Chinese Communist Party, the patriotic democratic parties, patriots without party affiliation, delegates from various people's organizations, and specially invited delegates.

In September 1949, exercising the functions and powers of the National People's Congress, the First Plenary Session of the CPPCC proclaimed the founding of the People's Republic of China. Since the First National People's Congress was conven-

ed in 1954, the CPPCC has continued to make great contributions to the nation's political life, social life and foreign affairs work.

The CPPCC is a major vehicle for the supervision and implementation of democracy in China. More specifically, it has helped to implement the policy of "long-term co-existence and mutual supervision" between the Chinese Communist Party and the patriotic democratic parties. Guiding itself by the Constitution of the People's Republic of China and its own regulations. the CPPCC holds consultations and offers opinions and advice on important matters concerning national policy and the people's daily lives.

The CPPCC has a national committee and many local committees. The main tasks of the national and local committees are: to organize trips, investigations and research, gather first-hand information and give opinions and advice with a view to helping state organs to propagate and implement the Party's policies and improve their work. The CPPCC also cooperates with relevant units in the political, economic, cultural, educational, scientific and technological fields in gathering more ideas and talented people for the country's construction.

On June 4 to 22, 1983, the Sixth Session of the Fifth National Committee of the CPPCC was held in Beijing. Deng Yingchao was elected to be the Chairman of the Sixth National Committee of the CPPCC. Among the members of the Standing Committee, the percentage of the delegates from the democratic parties and pa-

The First Session of the 6th CPPCC on June 4, 1984

triots of various circles was increased to a total of 64 percent. At present, more than one-third of delegates came from literary and artistic circles. The number of delegates from minority nationalities, compatriots in Taiwan and overseas was increased. In recent years, some foreigners who work in China and have been naturalized as Chinese citizens have also become members of the committee.

## A LIST OF CHAIRMEN AND VICE-CHAIRMEN OF THE NATIONAL COMMITTEES OF ALL THE PREVIOUS CPPCC

*The first CPPCC:*

Chairman: Mao Zedong
Vice-chairmen:
Zhou Enlai, Li Jishen, Shen Junru, Guo Moruo, Chen Shutong

*The second:*

Honorary Chairman: Mao Zedong
Chairman: Zhou Enlai
Vice-Chairmen:
Soong Ching Ling, Dong Biwu, Li Jishen, Zhang Lan, Guo Moruo, Peng Zhen, Shen Junru, Huang Yanpei, He Xiangning, Li Weihan, Li Siguang, Chen Shutong, Zhang Bojun, Chen Jiageng

*The third:*

Honorary Chairman: Mao Zedong
Chairman: Zhou Enlai
Vice-Chairmen:
Peng Zhen, Li Jishen, Guo Moruo, Shen Junru, Huang Yanpei, Li Weihan, Li Siguang, Chen Shutong, Chen Jiageng, Burhan Shahidi, Chen Yi, Kang Sheng, Pagbalha Geleg Namgyai, Ngapoi Ngawang Jigme

*The fourth:*

Honorary Chairman: Mao Zedong
Chairman: Zhou Enlai
Vice-Chairmen:
Peng Zhen, Chen Yi, Ye Jianying, Huang Yanpei, Chen Shutong, Liu Lantao, Song Renqiong, Xu Bing, Gao Chongmin, Cai Tingkai, Wei Guoqing, Deng Zihui, Li Siguang, Fu Zuoyi, Teng Daiyuan, Xie Juezai, Shen Yanbing, Li Zhuchen, Pagbalha Geleg Namgyai, Xu Deheng, Li Dequan, Ma Xulun

*The fifth:*

Chairman: Deng Xiaoping
Vice-Chairmen:
  Ulanhu, Wei Guoqing, Peng Chong, Zhao Ziyang, Guo Moruo, Song Renqiong, Shen Yanbing, Xu Deheng, Ouyang Qian, Shi Liang, Zhu Yunshan, Kang Keqing, Ji Fang, Wang Shoudao, Yang Jingren, Zhou Jianren, Zhang Chong, Pagbalha Geleg Namgyai, Zhuang Xiquan, Hu Zi'ang, Rong Yiren, Tong Dizhou

*The sixth:*

Chairman: Deng Yingchao (F)
Vice-Chairmen:
  Yang Jingren, Liu Lantao, Lu Dingyi, Cheng Zihua, Kang Keqing, Ji Fang, Zhuang Xiquan, Pagbalha Geleg Namgyai, Hu Zi'ang, Wang Kunlun, Qian Changzhao, Dong Qiwu, Tao Shiyue, Zhou Shutao, Yang Chengwu, Xiao Hua, Chen Zaidao, Lü Zhengcao, Zhou Jianren, Zhou Peiyuan, Burhan Shahidi, Miao Yuntai, Wang Guangying, Deng Zhaoxiang, Fei Xiaotong, Zhao Puchu, Ye Shengtao, Qu Wu, Ba Jin

# THE EARLIEST AND BIGGEST ENCYCLOPEDIA IN THE WORLD

The first Chinese encyclopedia was the *Yongle Canon* in 22,877 sections, compiled by Xie Jin during the Yongle period (1403-1424) of the Ming dynasty and bound into 11,095 volumes. It contained articles on astronomy, literature, art, Confucian classics, historical records, technology, agronomy, medicine, religion and other subjects. It is one of the most valuable sources on ancient and medieval China and the earliest and biggest encyclopedia in the world.

The encyclopedia was too vast and cumbersome to publish in even limited runs. There was only an original set and one reproduction made in the Jiajing period (1522-1567) in the Ming dynasty. The original was destroyed by fire and only 200 volumes from the reproduction are now extant. In 1959, the China Publishing House published 730 sections from these remaining volumes by photolithographic process.

# POLITICAL PARTIES

## THE COMMUNIST PARTY OF CHINA

The Communist Party of China is the vanguard of the Chinese working class, the representative of the interests of the Chinese people and the force at the core leading China's cause of socialism. It takes Marxism-Leninism and Mao Zedong Thought as its guide to action with an ultimate goal to create a communist social system.

Since its founding on July 1, 1921 in Shanghai, the CPC has led the people in a prolonged struggle against imperialism, feudalism and bureaucrat-capitalism, and won victory in the new-democratic revolution and established the People's Republic of China in 1949.

At the present stage, the CPC's general task is to unite the people of all nationalities to achieve the modernization of industry, agriculture, national defense and science and technology and make China a culturally advanced and highly democratic socialist country.

In its relationship with China's eight democratic parties, the CPC follows a policy of long-term coexistence and mutual supervision. It is a kind of cooperative relationship between friendly, not opposition, parties.

## THE EIGHT DEMOCRATIC PARTIES

*1. The China Revolutionary Committee of the Kuomintang*

On New Year's Day of 1948, the Revolutionary Committee of the Kuomintang was formally established by patriotic democratic elements in the Kuomintang who have remained loyal to Dr. Sun Yat-sen's revolutionary ideas and were against the then reactionary regime. In November 1949, this organization and other patriotic elements within the Kuomintang held the Second Congress of the Democratic Wing of the Kuomintang, and combined to form a single organization which still went by the name of the Revolutionary Committee of the Kuomintang. Most of the members of the Revolutionary Committee of the Kuomintang are former

KMT members, as well as intellectuals from cultural, educational, medical and financial circles with previous associations with the KMT.

### 2. China Democratic League

The China Democratic League was founded in 1941 as the League of Democratic Political Groups. In 1944, a national congress was held during which its name was changed to the China Democratic League. In January 1948, the China Democratic League met in Hongkong and was reorganized. Most members of the China Democratic League are intellectuals in the cultural, educational and scientific fields.

### 3. China Democratic National Construction Association

The China Democratic National Construction Association originated during the War of Resistance Against Japan in a series of discussion meetings held by a group of national industrialists and businessmen in Chongqing. Their discussions revolved around the current political situation and questions of common concern. On December 12, 1945, the China Democratic National Construction Association was formally established, and held its first national congress in April of 1955. Most of its members are industrialists and businessmen, as well as a number of intellectuals associated with them.

### 4. China Association for Promoting Democracy

This association was founded in Shanghai in 1945 by intellectuals engaged in patriotic democratic activities. Most of its members are intellectuals from cultural, publishing and educational circles, the latter being mostly teachers in primary and secondary schools.

### 5. Chinese Peasants' and Workers' Democratic Party

Founded in Shanghai in 1930 by Deng Yanda as the Provisional Action Committee of the Kuomintang, it became the Action Committee for Chinese National Liberation in 1935. On February 2, 1947, it held its fourth national cadres conference in Shanghai, where its present name was formally adopted. Most of its members are professionals in the medical, pharmaceutical and health care fields.

### 6. China Zhi Gong Dang

The predecessor of the China Zhi Gong Dang was a society of Hongkong and overseas Chinese — the Hong Men Zhi Gong Tang. On October 10, 1925, this society held its first congress in San Francisco, during which its members formally announced the society's transformation into a political party, the Zhi Gong Dang. However, due to the outbreak of the War of Resistance Against Japan, the Zhi Gong Dang temporarily ceased its activities in 1937 shortly after its second congress. In 1946, the Zhi Gong Dang re-commenced activities in Hongkong, and in 1947 it held its third congress there. In 1950, the leadership of the Zhi Gong Dang moved the party from Hongkong to Guangzhou. The members of the party are mostly overseas Chinese who have returned to live in China.

## 7. Jiu San Society

The Jiu San Society originated in 1944 in Chongqing during the War of Resistance Against Japan with the founding of the Democracy and Science Forum by a group of intellectuals from cultural, educational and scientific circles. Later, this symposium gradually developed into a political organization representing China's academic circles and took the name Democracy and Science Society. On September 3, 1945, in commemoration of the victory in the international war against fascism, it adopted its present name ("Jiu San" means September 3 in Chinese). The society's members are mostly leading intellectuals from scientific and technological circles.

## 8. Taiwan Democratic Self-Government League

The Taiwan Democratic Self-Government League was established in November 1947, by a group of patriotic democratic activists from Taiwan Province. The members of the Taiwan Democratic Self-Government League are socially eminent natives of Taiwan Province who now reside on the Chinese mainland.

# THE FIRST COUNTRY IN THE WORLD THAT ADOPTED THE DECIMAL SYSTEM

China was the first country in the world that adopted the decimal system. As early as the fourth century B.C. the Chinese were proficient in the use of a decimal system, which, for all intents and purposes, is the same as that used today. China's use of the decimal system preceded India by 1,000 years. With regard to the role it played in aiding the advancement of human civilization, the invention is said to be second in importance only to the adoption of fire.

# CIVIL ADMINISTRATION

Civil administration is an important part of the work of the Chinese government. At present, the Ministry of Civil Administration undertakes responsibility for making living arrangements for demobilized servicemen, providing special care to disabled servicemen and the families of revolutionary martyrs, providing relief to disaster areas and a wide variety of other social welfare tasks. Every year the Ministry of Civil Administration provides for the living arrangements and welfare of more than 200 million people, including orphans, the aged, the physically disabled, the disaster stricken as well as the blind, deaf and dumb.

Between 1979 and 1983, the Ministry of Civil Administration took a census of all demobilized servicemen in China and determined their political and economic status. It also revised and improved the methods of distributing regular subsidies to the dependents of revolutionary martyrs and of aiding those dependents of conscribed servicemen who live in the countryside. In helping to make living arrangements for demobilized and disabled servicemen, the ministry has gathered rich experience in helping people promote production and better their own living conditions through labor.

With its vast area, every year in China regions inhabited by over 100 million people suffer from some form of natural disaster. In these areas, local branches of the Ministry of Civil Administration carry out the policy of encouraging people to tide themselves over disasters by engaging in production, besides making timely distributions of food, money and other relief supplies. This relief work not only safeguards the lives of the disaster victims but also enables local production to return to normal within a relatively short period of time.

In China's urban areas, the Ministry of Civil Administration operates welfare wards, orphanages and mental institutions to provide for those among the aged, physically disabled and mentally ill who are homeless and without means of support.

Some of the concrete measures taken to aid these people are as follows:

In caring for the elderly, the main work consists of allowing them to rest and recuperate and making appropriate living arrangements for them, including providing them with opportunities to engage in light labor.

For disabled children of normal intelligence, physical therapy and education are provided. When possible, orthopedic procedures and physical therapy are used to treat these children while they are being educated and taught practical skills to prepare them for future employment.

Efforts are made to train retarded or otherwise mentally deficient children to care for themselves and to engage in simple forms of labor and production.

In caring for the mentally ill, the main work consists of providing support and various kinds of therapy. Mental illnesses are treated by arranging for patients to engage in appropriate labor, by administering drugs, and by providing them with entertainment and educational activities.

By 1983, China had more than 10,000 comprehensive production enterprises for the disabled which provided employment for more than 70 percent of China's urban disabled.

In many countries, the blind, deaf, mute and physically handicapped are entirely dependent on social welfare and charity and many live a lonely life. In China, however, these people are given a chance to establish themselves socially by working in factories run by the various departments of civil administration. The government shows its concern for the success of these enterprises in many ways. According to law, these factories are tax exempt during the first year of operation. If necessary, they can apply for an extension of their tax exemption for the second year. In order to encourage factories to employ the disabled, Chinese law stipulates that factories wherein more than 35 percent of the workers are disabled are permanently exempt from paying income taxes. These factories regularly invest a portion of their profits in expanding production, and use the remaining profits to improve the lives of their disabled staff members. The Chinese government provides throughout the country numerous forms of support for these factories, such as giving them top priority in providing supplies and guaranteeing the sales of their products.

In China, the blind, deaf, mute and physically disabled enjoy the same social standing as members of the rest of the population. Certain disabled people have even risen to positions of social prominence. To cite some examples, Han Qixiang, although blind, is simultaneously a representative to the National People's Congress and the Chairman of the China Folk Performing Art Association, while Huang Nai, though deaf and mute, is a member of the Chinese People's Political Consultative Conference.

A Blind Worker at Work

# THE INVENTION OF GUNPOWDER

China invented gunpowder made from nitre, sulphur and charcoal between 220 and 280 A.D. By about the 10th century, the use of gunpowder was common in the Huanghe River valley. Emperor Zhenzong of the Song dynasty (998-1022) set up a factory for the manufacture of gunpowder of three distinct types at Kaifeng. This was the earliest sophisticated use of gunpowder in the world. In about the 12th or 13th century, gunpowder was introduced to Greece and Europe via the Middle East.

At first gunpowder was not used as a weapon but to power rockets and firecrackers for the pleasure of spectators. It was later developed not only for military use, but for blasting mountains, civil engineering and mining. Now, gunpowder plays an important role in industry and agriculture.

# EMPLOYMENT AND WAGE SYSTEMS

## 1. SYSTEMS OF EMPLOYMENT

The following are the major systems of employment in China:

### 1) Permanent job system

Workers hired within quotas fixed in the national economic plan which determines increases in the number of workers are considered permanently employed. This system is the major employment system in state-owned and collective enterprises, and offers workers the benefits of job security.

### 2) Temporary system

In this system, employers and workers sign a contract in which time periods, working conditions, and compensation are stipulated. Workers in this system are called contract workers. A work plan is usually made at the time of recruitment.

### 3) Seasonal job system

Seasonal enterprises such as sugar refineries, tea plantations, and fruit processing plants, in which the work is concentrated in short periods of time, hire large numbers of seasonal workers. Such enterprises also provide permanent occupations for a small number of specialized laborers and maintenance workers. Seasonal workers generally work in factories during the production season and return to the farms when their services are no longer required.

### 4) Worker-peasant system

In this system, peasants engage in agricultural work during the busy season and work in other areas during the slack season. This system is utilized predominantly in enterprises owned by communes or production teams, and occasionally in county-run enterprises. In those periods when peasants are engaged in non-agricultural labor, their status as commune member remains unchanged.

### 5) Other employment systems

Production tasks and the requisite materials are given to collectives or individual workers. The standards and other conditions required for the products are stipulated in a contract. Workers can work collectively or individually at home. This system covers such handicraft industries as weaving, embroidery and drawn work.

In a variation of the aforementioned system, work is distributed to collectives or individuals but is carried out at the site of the enterprise. This system is often used for assembly or packing.

A system of shifts serves as the framework for contracts signed between enterprises and people's communes or production brigades. Commune members alternate working in factories and returning to the countryside according to fixed schedules. This system is frequently adopted in the case of stenuous or potentially harmful jobs.

## 2. THE MANAGEMENT OF THE LABOR FORCE

The management of the labor force comprises the organization, deployment and utilization of able-bodied workers. It includes hiring, training, mobilization, inspection and testing, reward and punishment, and dismissal.

Young workers are assigned to jobs to meet the needs of all sectors of the economy. All graduates of colleges, universities and secondary schools are assigned jobs by the government according to a unified employment program. High school and junior high school students and other jobless youths are assigned work according to the "three-in-one"

## THE COUNTRY WHICH ORIGINATED SERICULTURE AND SILK-WEAVING

China has the longest history of silk production of any country in the world, and its output of silk has historically always been the largest. Chinese sericulture techniques and silkworm seeds were transmitted to Korea in about the 12th century B.C. and from there traveled to Japan in the third century A.D. Chinese sericulture techniques were introduced to Iran, Afghanistan, Iraq and Central Asia in the fourth century and to Greece in 550 A.D. The technology of silk manufacture was passed from Southwest Asia to France in the 15th century and within one hundred years it had spread throughout all of Europe.

employment policy.* Workers with no specialized training will be apprenticed for a period of one to three years after entering the enterprises.

Beginning in 1980, the system of "open hiring and selecting the best applicants" has been adopted in certain areas. This system operates as follows:

1) Following a state-approved labor plan, an employer will make a public announcement of the qualifications, the type of work and compensation for the available jobs. Unemployed people may apply for any available jobs according to their own interests and special skills.

2) The applicants will then be examined morally, intellectually and physically and the best applicants will be selected.

3) Newly hired workers are subject to a period of probation at the conclusion of which they may be dismissed if their performance is unsatisfactory.

4) If employees are not satisfied with their work, they may resign and find other jobs.

In April 1982, the State Council issued the "Rules for the Staff and Workers of Enterprises" which apply to all employees in state-owned enterprises and collective enterprises in the cities and towns. Regarding rewards, the "Rules" stipulate that moral encouragement should be combined with material rewards, with an emphasis on the former; and that ideological education should take precedence over other forms of punishment when discipline is violated. Monetary rewards are granted along with different types of moral encouragement while fines imposed in addition to various punishments. The "Rules" also specify the fines to be imposed for breaches of discipline.

## 3. SYSTEM OF WAGE SCALE

The wage system based on the principle of "from each according to his ability and to each according to his work" comprises the wage scale system, bonuses and miscellaneous subsidies. The income from these three sources constitutes the total wage income of an employee.**

The wage scale in state-owned enterprises and official organs is formulated and issued by the Central Government.

---

* To provide jobs in state, collective and private units.

** That portion of a worker's wages which is paid according to the wage scale is called the standard wage, and is the principal form of cashincome received by workers. Awards play a supplementary role, while subsidies make up for any deficiencies.

The wages of workers and staff members in collectives are set by the local authorities or enterprises at levels equal to or somewhat lower than those in state-owned enterprises.

*1) Workers' wage scale system*

Wage scales in China are set on an industry to industry basis. In the same city, however, workers such as drivers and cooks, whose occupations are common to nearly all industries, are paid according to a unified wage scale.

A system of eight grades applies to most workers, and a seven-grade system has been adopted to a lesser extent in such areas as the building industry.

The wage scale system for workers is composed of three elements: technical grades, the wage scale table and wage standards (or wage rate).

Technical grades are fixed according to the technical complexity, the degree of precision and the amount of responsibility involved in each type of work. The technical grade determines the place of each type of work in the wage scale table. Each technical grade requires a specific amount of technical knowledge on the part of the workers, a given level of operating ability, and particular technical standards.

The wage scale table includes wage rates and wage scale coefficients, and fixes wage grades for different types of work. The wage grade coefficients include proportional coefficients, progressive proportional coefficients and irregular coefficients with proportional coefficients being implemented in most cases. At present, the highest wage in the eight-grade wage system is 3 times greater than the lowest wage. In a few enterprises, this ratio can be as high as 3.2 to 1, and in other enterprises which call for comparatively simple technical skills, the ratio may be lower than 3 to 1.

Cash wages are paid out as compensation for labor performed over a period of time. In general, workers receive their wages on a monthly basis, with the daily wage being figured on the basis of 25.5 days per month, deducting the 7 official holidays and 52 Sundays in a year:

$$\frac{365 \ (\text{days}) - 7 \ (\text{holidays} - 52 \ (\text{Sundays})}{12 \ (\text{months})} = 25.5 \ (\text{days})$$

## THE BIGGEST STONE BUDDHA

A Maitreya Buddha was carved in a rock to the confluence of Minjiang River, Dadu River and Qingyi River in front of southeast Lingyun Mountain in Leshan County, Sichuan Province, in Tang dynasty from the first year of Kaiyuan to the 19th year of Zhenyuan (713-803 A.D.). The Buddha is 71 meters high and is the biggest stone Buddha in China. It is 18 meters higher than the Miyang Buddha in Afghanistan. The head of Buddha is about 10 meters in height. A foot of the Buddha can possess more than 100 persons standing on it. Two persons can sit side by side on a toenail of the Buddha.

### 2) Staff members' wage scale system

A wage system based on occupations is adopted for engineers, technicians and management personnel in state-owned enterprises and administrative staff in government organs.

The occupation-based wage system promulgated in 1956 divided all industries — such as manufacturing, capital construction and transportation — into four types. Offices in each enterprise were again classified into three types according to their importance and complexity. People working in these offices were similarly divided into several kinds. China was divided into seven economic zones. This complex, somewhat irrational, system was revised in 1963 by doing away with the classification of offices and specific enterprises, and simplified into a unified wage scale system based on actual wage levels. Some departments have created two different wage scales with 17 grades each, one for engineers and technicians and the other for administrative personnel. The highest wage on this scale is more than 9 times greater than the lowest wage.

### 3) Wage Readjustments

In 1955, administrative personnel in state organs were divided into 11 different zones and a wage system of 30 grades based on occupations was implemented. The highest wage was 31.1 times greater than the lowest wage, with grade one being the highest. In the following years, the wages of high officials were reduced on three occasions and the lowest wage level was raised. At present, a system of 24 grades is in effect wherein the highest wage is around 12 times greater than the lowest.

From 1949 to 1956, a system of regular promotion was adopted for workers. This system was part of the annual wage fund plan. Workers could apply for promotion and undergo assessment based on the technical standards of the work grade they were seeking. If they attained the required technical standards and operating skills, they would be promoted to the appropriate post with a corresponding higher wage. Promotions of engineers, technicians and administrative personnel were also subject to approval by the masses and the leadership of the enterprises.

After the second reform of the national wage system in 1956, regular promotion of workers was discontinued. Promotions were granted only three times — in 1959, 1963 and 1971 — in the twenty years from 1957 to 1977. Only two

Self-trained Tailors, One of the Most Popular Private Occupations, at the Tailors' Quarter of a Free Market

percent of all workers were promoted in 1959. A long period with no promotions created a situation in which workers' wages were no longer sufficient to compensate workers for their technical abilities and actual performance. Since 1977, the government has been increasingly concerned with the problem of workers' promotion. In the six years between 1977 and 1982, promotions for workers and staff members were carried out five times, and a total of 80 percent of all workers and staff members promoted during this period. At the same time, general assessments of workers, engineers, technicians and administrative personnel were made, providing important data for the future promotions of these workers and staff members.

## 4. SUBSIDY SYSTEM

According to statistics compiled in 1978, there are more

than 200 different kinds of subsidy systems being implemented in China. Subsidies are not necessarily related to wages; they may be financed from wage funds; they may be included in production costs; they may be appropriated from welfare benefits; or they may be covered by appropriations from state funds. Some subsidies are enjoyed by only a few workers, and others by all. Some subsidies are fixed on a nationwide basis by the government or by an enterprise's own trade union or local trade unions. The following are the more widespread subsidy systems now in effect:

1) Subsidies to workers and staff members in outlying districts or in special environments. For example, subsidies for workers in coal mines were initiated in the 1950s. Also in this category are subsidies for workers in forestry, geological prospecting, iron and steel mills, hydroelectric projects and the construction of new railways.

2) Workers and staff members' overtime subsidies. This category includes overtime payments, night-shift subsidies for scientific and technical personnel who give lectures outside of their regular work.

3) Subsidies to cover living costs during periods of leave. Such subsidies are provided when workers or staff members leave their posts to fulfill government or social obligations; when they stop working for reasons beyond their own control; when they are assigned to advanced study by the enterprises; and when they visit their parents or relatives in accordance with fixed regulations.

4) Rewards to a small number of workers who have made special contributions in production or service. These include technical subsidies, occupational subsidies, teachers' subsidies, and commercial and service trades subsidies.

5) Subsidies to reduce the living expenses of workers and staff members. These include subsidies for winter heating, commuting to and from work, purchasing grain and other food items, and for accommodating the special dietary needs of Moslems.

## 5. THE AWARD SYSTEM

*1) Nature and development of the system*

As a supplement to the regular wage scale system, the award system reinforces the socialist principle "to each according to his work" by offering a range of bonuses to workers engaged in the same trades with identical wage scales in the light of the workers' actual performance.

The system was established on the basis of the wage scale system in 1952. It integrates spiritual and material awards, though the latter were suspended in 1958 shortly after the Great Leap Forward, and again during the "cultural revolution" (1966-1976). Material awards were not reinstated until 1978.

At present, most Chinese enterprises and establishments follow a system of giving production bonuses or wage bonuses on a monthly base. Such bonuses may be based on a comprehensive assessment of a worker's fulfillment of all his or her production quotas, or on his or her fulfillment or over-fulfillment of a production quota specified in the state plan, while the latter encourages increased output, improvements in the product quality, or economizing on materials. Enterprises may adopt either or both of the two forms according to their individual circumstances.

Besides the regular production bonuses, provisional bonuses are awarded to ac-knowledge inventions, constructive suggestions or the retrieval of recyclable goods in the course of production. Examples of the latter are construction workers retrieving cement bags, and miners recovering timber and steel props used in the mines. Hand in hand with monetary bonuses are various spiritual awards conferred on exemplary individuals and groups. Titles for the former include Advanced Laborer, Model Worker, and Quality Pacesetter, and for the latter, Advanced Production Group, Model Workshop, and Advanced Enterprise. These titles are awarded in the form of certificates of merits, medals or brocade banners.

2) *Sources of bonuses*

In general, state wage funds provide for regular production bonuses, though in some cases they are part of production costs. As part of recent experiments wherein enterprises retain part of their profits for their own use or assume sole responsibility for their own profits and losses, and enterprises may apportion some of their retained profits for bonuses. Bonuses for economizing on materials are derived from savings gained in the process. Special state funds cover bonuses which are not related to production.

### 3) Level of bonuses

When setting the levels of monthly bonuses, the state follows the principle of "simultaneously protecting the interests of the state, collective and individual".

Despite several setbacks in the course of implementing the bonus system, the level of bonuses has risen consistently. In the early 1950s, monthly bonuses averaged three to five percent of workers' monthly wages. Between 1956 and 1966, before the period of the "cultural revolution", bonuses were equal to around eight percent of workers' monthly wages in enterprises and three percent in commercial and service trades. At present, bonuses average 16 to 25 percent of workers' monthly wages, which means that a worker's annual bonuses may amount to two or three months' salary.

## THE WORLD'S LONGEST SERIES OF BOOKS

In 1772, Qianlong, the fourth emperor of the Qing dynasty, ordered that a literary selection be compiled based on the most important texts in the four traditional divisions of Chinese learning — classical works, historical works, philosophical works and belles-lettres. The work which resulted, the *Si Ku Quan Shu* (Complete Library in the Four Branches of Literature), was compiled over a ten year period between 1772-1782 and involved the scrutiny of entire libraries, both imperial and private, by a small army of scholars. This work originally contained 3,503 titles which were bound into 79,337 volumes with over 997 million words (portions of the work were later lost to fire or destroyed during the depredations by the military expeditions of the foreign powers in China during the latter part of the 19th century). Nevertheless, at the time of its completion the work made a signal contribution to the cataloguing and preservation of Chinese literature, and was also the world's longest single unified interconnected series of books.

# SENIOR CITIZENS

In China, people 60 years of age or older are considered senior citizens. In 1980, there were 80 million senior citizens, making up eight percent of the population; by 2025, this number will rise to 280 million, or 20 percent of the population. At present, there are 100 million elder folk, or ten percent of China's population. In view of these large numbers, a National Elderly Citizens' Committee was established in April of 1983.

"Treating the elderly with respect regardless of whether they are members of one's own family" is an important part of traditional Chinese ethics. China's retirement system, social welfare plan, medical insurance programs and special physical education activities are designed to ensure that senior citizens spend their remaining years in happiness. The total state expenditure on pensions is approximately six billion yuan a year.

Preparing Meat-Dumpling at a Senior Citizens' Home

Throughout the Chinese countryside, there are 2.2 million childless widows and widowers and unmarried older people enjoying the "Five Guarantees" — food, housing, clothing, medical treatment and burial — while in the cities some 140,000 senior citizens live in more than nine thousand homes for the aged. Partially due to such provisions for the elderly, the average life span in China has increased from 35 years in 1949 to 69 years in 1980.

In recent years, China has established a Senior Citizens' Athletic Association, while the Chinese Academy of Social Sciences has set up a research organization devoted to the study of older people. The magazine *Elderly Chinese* is being published on a national scale, and in the near future a foundation will be established whose work will be of benefit to China's older people.

Beijing Hospital now has a research institute for geriatric diseases and is in the process of setting up special clinics and rehabilitation centers for the aged. Similar facilities have also been provided in Shanghai and Guangzhou.

## THE WORLD'S MOST ANCIENT HANDWRITTEN NEWSPAPER

The world's most ancient handwritten newspaper dates back from the third year of Guangqi (887) of the Tang dynasty. The paper is 97 cm. long and 34 cm. wide and contains over 2,000 neatly written characters in 60 lines, with a general heading of four characters reading "Presenting a Memorial to the Throne". The newspaper contains a report as to how Governor Zhang Huaishen, an official in the late Tang dynasty, who governed 11 counties in the vicinity of Dunhuang in what is today's Gansu Province, dispatched his envoy to the imperial court to ask for a tally. This newspaper was published 700 years earlier than the earliest Western newspaper. In the early 20th century the paper was robbed from the Mogao Grotto of the Dunhuang Caves and is now on display in the library of the British Museum in London.

# ACCELERATING URBAN CONSTRUCTION

In the four years between 1979 and 1982, some 380 million square meters of housing were built in China's cities and towns, providing housing for a total of 7.8 million households, or 31 million persons, and representing fully 70 percent of all housing built between 1949 and 1978.

In the same period, China's urban population grew by 22.2 million, an average annual increase of 5.6 million. This population increase combined with the overall development of urban industry has left nearly one-third of China's urban residents in need of improved housing.

At present, China has a total of 289 cities, more than twice the number at the time of the founding of the People's Republic. These cities together with the nation's some 2,800 towns are the home of China's 142.9 million urban population. The 890 million square meters of housing constructed in these areas from 1949 to 1982 represent 2.7 times the total area of housing available in urban China in 1949, while the urban population itself has increased 2.47 times during the same period.

Out of the above-mentioned 289 cities, 20 have populations of one million or more, 28 have populations of 500,000 to one million, 71 have populations of 200,000 to 500,000 and 170 have populations of less than 200,000.

In order to speed up urban construction and improve people's housing conditions, the Chinese government has recently adopted a policy of making full use of the initiative and resources of both localities and individuals, discarding its pre-1977 policy of being the sole investor in all urban housing construction. Now whenever the central or local government establishes an enterprise, a special appropriation for residential housing is included in the project's overall budget. Furthermore, industrial enterprises may now use part of their retained profits or welfare funds for housing construction. Individuals are now encouraged to buy or build private houses.

At present, in the four cities of Zhengzhou (Henan), Changzhou (Jiangsu), Shashi (Hubei) and Siping (Liaoning), the state is experimenting with helping individuals to build their own homes by paying for two-thirds of the construction expenses with the future home owners paying the remaining third.

At the same time, China has taken strict measures to control the growth of population in the larger cities and has made vigorous efforts to speed construction in its small cities and

Constructions in Beijing

towns. In general, major construction projects are no longer built in large cities but rather in smaller cities and the satellite towns encircling the large cities.

The state encourages the industrial sector to build factories in small cities and towns and to improve housing, cultural, educational, medical, recreational and shopping facilities in these areas. Many small cities and towns have gradually grown into medium-sized cities. The most outstanding examples are Daqing, an oil-producing city in Heilongjiang Province; Shiyan in Hubei Province, a center of China's automobile industry, and Dukou in Sichuan Province, the site of a major metallurgical industrial complex.

Increased efforts are being made to upgrade urban infrastructure and essential daily services. The annual consumption of water by China's urban residents and industries stands at approximately 30 billion cubic meters, representing a 20-fold increase as compared with 1949. Nevertheless, at present only about half of all of China's cities and towns have running water, the remainder obtaining their supply from wells equipped with electric pumps, diesel pumps and manual pumps and, from traditional wells.

The annual non-industrial consumption of electricity in China's urban areas is 15 billion kilowatts, a mere 5.5 percent of the country's total, and gas facilities are available only in a few large cities. Therefore, coal is still the most commonly used form of fuel in China's urban areas, their combined annual coal consumption amounting to as much as 50 million tons. This heavy reliance on coal as a source of power combined with China's recent giant strides towards industrialization has combined to give rise to an increasingly serious urban air pollution problem. However, the Chinese government has already taken measures to combat it, such as promulgating a recent Environmental Protection Law.

The planting of flowers, trees and grass in the cities, with an end to both beautifying and protecting the urban environment, is taking place on a large scale throughout the country. In this respect, Beijing is a model for all Chinese cities, though residents of Tianjin and Xi'an have also voluntarily participated in helping to build more public parks in their cities.

# POSTAL AND TELECOMMUNICATIONS SERVICES

In China, the two separate services of the post and telecommunications both come under the leadership of a single organization, the Ministry of Posts and Telecommunications. The postal bureau is in charge of the collection and delivery of the mail, the distribution of newspapers and periodicals, and the forwarding of remittances. The telecommunications bureau provides the nation with telephone, telegraph, telex and radiophotography services and also handles data transmission.

A postal service was established in China as early as the Shang dynasty (c. 16th-11th centuries B.C.), but at that time the service had no fixed name. It was not until the Zhou dynasty (c. 11th century-221 B.C.) that the service became known by the fixed appellation "post". To more effectively supervise the feudal fiefdoms it presided over, the central government created a network of new postal roads and repaired those already ex-

tant. Moreover, along every major road and thoroughfare it established mail forwarding stations and appointed people the tasks of collecting, transmitting and delivering the mail.

In 221 B.C., the First Emperor of the Qin dynasty unified China under his rule and carried further the work of establishing a complete communications network throughout the kingdom. He made laws stipulating that the axial length of all wheeled vehicles in his kingdom be a uniform 169.50 centimeters, that all postal roads in the country be uniformly 50 paces wide, and that postal stations be established every five kilometers along their length. These laws assigned local officials the task of administering these postal stations and ensuring the delivery of the mail, staffing each station with postal messengers, and supplying horses and carts for mail delivery. The entire postal system was furthermore governed by a set of strict administrative regulations and sanctions.

Prior to the Ming dynasty (1368-1644), postal stations in China transmitted mail exclusively between officials and local government authorities, and provided for the conveyance of official documents and reports on the military situation at the nation's borders; they did not transmit private correspondence or letters between ordinary citizens. It was not until the middle days of the Ming dynasty that an organization was formed for delivering private correspondence. This bureau commenced by delivering letters, remittances and packages, and later expanded its services to include the distribution of newspapers and books. The first Chinese newspaper to be distributed by mail was the *Di Bao*, or *Capital Gazette*, which was published in the Han dynasty (206 B.C.-220 A.D.)

In 1866, the Qing government established a postal service office under the Customs Revenue Department, and in 1896 formally established a postal bureau. In 1911, the customs and postal bureaus were separated and the postal bureau became an independent administrative unit.

Today, the Chinese Posts and Telecommunications Bureau has numerous offices and the scope of operations is vast: its communications lines reach the remotest corners of the country. The bureau makes use of the full range of modern communications and delivery methods to serve the myriad households throughout China, and utilize its extensive communications network to distribute newspapers and periodicals to Chinese readers. In March 1950 and in early 1953, the Ministry of Posts and Telecommunications took on the responsibility of distributing Chinese periodicals. Every year the ministry publishes a catalog of newspapers and periodicals to which readers can subscribe. Newspapers and periodicals are also retailed throughout China in posts and telecommunications offices and branch post offices, retail sales outlets and newspaper kiosks. At present, more than 600 specialized newspaper and periodical sales outlets have been established in China's cities and towns.

The number of newspapers and magazines has also increased over the years. For the convenience of foreign travelers and tourists in China, outlets

Postal Workers on Their Daily Delivery Rounds

selling domestically published foreign language books, magazines and newspapers have been opened in hotels and spots of touristic interest throughout the country.

In international communications, China has direct postal connections with 111 countries and regions and express mail delivery connections with 15 countries and regions. China has established telecommunications connections with 120 countries and regions and has direct electronic linkups with 46 countries and regions. It also makes direct television and radio broadcasts to several major countries.

In response to the needs of foreign businessmen and domestic consumers, on September 9, 1980, China officially established telex and facsimile transmission services for individual users in China. Using communications lines connected to China's telecommunications offices, customers can transmit telegraphic and telex messages directly from their own offices and residences, and can also transmit diagrams, photographs and documents.

On July 15, 1980, the Ministry of Posts and Telecommunications established international express mail delivery services from Beijing, Shanghai,

Tianjin, Guangzhou, Fuzhou and Shenzhen. Furthermore, commencing May 21, 1981, the ministry resumed using service code and the standard international language of communications.

In order to bridge the communications gap between China and the rest of the world, in the June-October period of 1982, China established a total of ten ground satellite stations in Beijing, Shanghai, Nanjing, Chengdu, Shijiazhuang as well as in Xinjiang and Inner Mongolia. A series of domestic telecommunications and television broadcast tests were conducted and achieved the expected results. Of these ten stations, nine have already received permission to participate in the international telecommunications network.

In the near future, in addition to developing its own communications satellite system, China will also carry out the construction of the Beijing International Communications Center. When completed, the center will provide Beijing with an automatic international telephone dialing system and facilitate the sending and receiving of international telegrams.

## THE WORLD'S BIGGEST STAMP

Stamps are not only merely certificates indicating that a certain amount of postage fees has been paid, but are also objects of considerable cultural and historical interest.

The first stamp which China ever issued was printed in 1878 and featured a dragon head, hence it was referred to as the "dragon head". Another stamp which China issued in 1913 for express mail measures 247.5 mm. long and 69.8 mm. wide, making it the biggest stamp ever printed in the world.

# EDUCATION

Beginning in the Western Zhou dynasty (c. 11th century B.C.-770 B.C.) government-run imperial colleges were established in China. During the Spring and Autumn and Warring States periods (770-207 B.C.) scholar sages, such as Confucius and Mencius, gave private lessons to groups of selected disciples.

In 1840, after its defeat in the Opium War, China became increasingly exposed to Western educational practices. The number of missionary schools directly controlled by foreign powers increased rapidly, gradually forming an independent educational system within the country. By the late 19th century, the tottering Qing government started to implement educational reforms by transforming some of the traditional educational academies into modern government-run schools offering Western subjects as part of their curricula. After the 1911 Revolution, China began to develop a Western-style system encompassing all levels of education from primary school to college. Prior to 1949, in addition to government-run educational institutions, there were a great number of missionary schools and privately-run institutions.

On the eve of Liberation, the entire nation had only 200 institutions of higher learning, 4,000 middle schools and 289,000 primary schools. Only 20 percent of all children of primary school age were enrolled in school and 80 percent of the population was illiterate.

After the founding of the People's Republic in 1949, the People's Government made fundamental changes in the old educational system. It took over all the public and private schools of the former regime and incorporated all former missionary schools into the national educational system. The government also implemented a policy of facilitating enrollment for the children of workers and peasants, and established organizations for carrying out political and ideological work throughout the entire educational system.

After 1952, the Chinese government made necessary adjustments in its educational system with regard to the universities and their departments and commenced the implementation of united systems of university admissions and work assignment after graduation. After 1957, the Ministry of Education commenced implementing the policy that "everyone who receives an education" should be enabled to "develop morally, intellectually and physically and become professionally competent socialist-minded workers". After 1960, the ministry continued to effect reforms throughout the entire educational system in terms of curricula, teaching, scientific research, productive labor and ideological education. The ensuing five-year period witnessed a notable improvement in many spheres. However, with the commencement of the "cultural revolution" in 1966, unprecedented harm was wreaked on the educational system, reducing much of it to a shambles. Many schools were closed throughout the nation and the majority of teachers were maligned and subjected to ruthless persecution. Throughout China the quality of education dropped precipitously.

After the overthrow of the Gang of Four in 1976, the Chinese educational system underwent a four-year period of reform and by 1980 it was once again back on the path of healthy development. By 1981, there were 704 universities and institutions of higher learning, 112,505 secondary schools (including junior middle schools and technical secondary schools), and 894,074 primary schools. Approximately 93 percent of all children of school age were enrolled.

According to China's 1982 census, among China's population of 1,008,175,288 persons spread throughout its 29 provinces, autonomous regions and municipalities directly under the Central Government, there are presently 4,414,495 college graduates as well as 1,602,474 persons who are either currently at college or who left college before graduation, 66,478,028 senior middle school graduates, 178,277,140 junior middle school graduates, and an additional 355,160,310 persons who have attended primary schools. These figures for China's senior and junior middle schools and primary schools include graduates, persons still in school, and persons who left school without graduating. Illiterate and semi-literate persons account for a total of 23.3 percent of the population.

## PRESCHOOL EDUCATION

There are two types of kindergartens in China: those run by the state and those run by the local people. These further subdivide into overnight, day and half-day kindergartens. Kindergarten children are grouped into three classes according to their ages; 3-4 year olds comprising the beginners' class, 4-5 years olds comprising the intermediate class, and 5-6 year olds comprising the advanced class. Within each kindergarten there is usually a nursery to take care of the 2-3 year old toddlers. The kindergartens provide instruction in such subjects as language, general knowledge of life and the environment, simple calculation, music, fine arts and physical culture. The number of class hours per week varies· according to the age of the children: six periods a week for the beginners' class, each lasting 15 minutes; 12 periods a week for the intermediate class, each lasting 25 minutes; and 14 periods a week for the advanced class, each lasting 35 minutes.

The task of the kindergartens is to cultivate good habits in the children so as to ensure their healthy development in mind and body, and further to assist them in acquiring the fine moral qualities of honesty, bravery, cooperation, friendliness, discipline and politeness. Kindergartens also cultivate an interest in language, calculation, art and music in their children.

In 1979, a supervisory body was especially established to take charge of nursery and kindergarten work. The membership of this organization is composed of leading cadres from 13 ministries and organizations, including representatives of the Ministry of Education, the Ministry of Finance, the All-China Women's Federation and the Chinese Society for the Protection of Children. Several of China's largest cities, including Beijing and Shanghai, established a Children's Press to meet the need for children's books and periodicals. One of the leading publications is *Reading Through Pictures*, a great favorite among children readers.

## PRIMARY EDUCATION

Since the establishment of the People's Republic, the government has consistently emphasized the importance of the popularization of primary education and at present it has already become universal almost in the whole country.

Primary education consists of a six-year period of study,

and the average age of the children at entrance is between six and seven. In primary schools 40 weeks a year are devoted to study (including four weeks for reviews and examination), 10 weeks for summer and winter vacations and two weeks for miscellaneous activities. During the agricultural busy season pupils in the countryside are given extra time off to provide supplementary labor service in the production teams or at home.

Primary school pupils attend between 24 and 27 hours of classes per week. Curricula include ethics, Chinese, arithmatics, natural science, geography, history, music, physical culture and fine arts. In primary schools the time allotted for class meetings, private study, manual labor and other extracurricular activities generally does not exceed six hours a week.

## SECONDARY EDUCATION

Aided by the popularization of primary school education, middle school education has also seen considerable development in recent years and junior middle school education has already become popularized in many of China's cities.

There are two levels of secondary education: three years of junior middle school education and three years of senior middle school education. In order to enter senior middle schools students must first pass an entrance examination. For each academic year 40 weeks are devoted to academic learning, leaving 10 to 11 weeks for summer and winter vacations, holidays and festivals. In addition, four weeks are set aside for physical labor and technical training. Junior middle school students attend between 30 and 31 hours of class per week and senior middle school students attend 29 hours of class per week. The time allotted for extracurricular activities generally does not exceed seven hours.

The courses offered in junior middle schools include Chinese, mathematics, foreign language, politics, history, geography, biology, physics, chemistry, physiology and physical culture, music and fine arts. The courses offered in senior middle schools include Chinese, mathematics, foreign language, politics, physics, chemistry, biology, history, geography and physical culture.

In order to meet the needs of the country's modernization program, the Chinese government is currently in the midst of reforming its secondary edu-

A University Language Lab.

cational system and is gradually reviving secondary technical schools as well as a variety of other specialized secondary professional schools.

## HIGHER EDUCATION

There are 12 kinds of institutions of higher learning in China: comprehensive universities, colleges and universities of engineering, agriculture, forestry, medical science, teachers' training, business administration and economics, political science and law, physical culture, arts, foreign languages and minority nationalities. Comprehensive universities have two colleges: liberal arts and sciences. A college of liberal arts generally has the following departments: languages, literature, history, philosophy, economics and law. A college of sciences has, generally speaking, the departments of mathematics, physics, chemistry, biology, geography, geology, radio, electronics and others. Beijing, Nankai and Fudan universities are examples of comprehensive universities.

There are two kinds of engineering colleges or universities. One is the multi-discipline engineering college or university that has many engineering departments besides the school of sciences. Qinghua University is a good example of this kind of university. Its departments include construction engineering, water conservancy, chemical engineering, computer engineering and thermal engineering. The other is the single-discipline engineering college, such as the colleges of mining, iron and steel, geology, petroleum and chemical engineering.

In China's institutions of higher education, the period of study is generally four or five years, with certain special schools, such as medical schools, having longer periods of study, and certain technical schools offering two- or three-year programs of study. But only academic institutions requiring four or more years of study issue college diplomas to their graduates, institutes requiring only two or three years of study merely issuing graduation certificates.

Students in Chinese institutions of higher learning enjoy free tuition, free medical treatment and free lodging and board, and are asked only to make small contributions towards their food and teaching material expenses. Students in financial difficulty receive extra subsidies, including food expenses. Those studying at normal colleges or universities or minority nationality institutes do not have to pay anything at all. Those who have worked for more than five years prior to their enrollment in colleges will continue to receive pay from their former work units and in this case, the state provides no direct financial aid.

In order to train high-level specialized personnel for training or research in the institutions of higher learning, China has established postgraduate studies programs in 316 of its institutions of higher learning. The length of study for postgraduates varies from two to four years. On January 1, 1981, Chinese institutions commenced granting academic degrees. College graduates receive a bachelor's degree, while postgraduates may be candidates for either an M.A. or Ph.D. degree.

China has more than 50 colleges and universities which have developed various types of academic and scholarly exchange with universities abroad. More than 30 universities have entered agreements with universities abroad to engage in the exchange of students and scholars. In addition, sizable numbers of foreign teachers and professors have been invited to China to teach foreign languages or to give lectures on science and technology. Meanwhile, institutions of higher learning in China have been sending an increasing number of scholars and professors abroad to give lectures, to do research and to take part in international conferences.

## ADULT EDUCATION

In addition to educating its young people, the Chinese government also lays emphasis on adult education, including peasants' education, education to workers and staff members, education by radio and TV, and correspondence school and evening university. Of all these types of adult education, televised instruction has witnessed the most rapid advancement in recent years.

The TV University was jointly established in 1979 by the Ministry of Education and the Broadcasting Administration Bureau (now named the Ministry of Radio and Television Broadcasting). This university is open to all persons who pass the preliminary entrance exam and obtain their work units' permission to enroll. Its courses are intended for persons who have achieved at least a senior middle school level of education, and its student body includes many workers and staff members, school teachers, and urban and rural educated youth. At present, the curriculum of TV University includes basic general-purpose courses in science and technology as well as more specialized high-level courses in advanced mathematics, physics, chemistry, engineering, mechanics, fundamentals of computer science and computer language, biology and English. It takes the TV University three years to complete the transmission of each of the courses offered. The students of the TV University have three different statuses: students who take the full load of four courses, those who take two courses and those who take one course. They study on a full-time, part-time and spare-time basis respectively.

Workers and staff members who have received permission from their work units to study in TV University are paid their normal wage or salary. Full-time students are released from their work during the entire duration of their study, those who take two courses are permitted to work half-time and those who take a single course generally do so in their spare-time. The expenses for most of the students' books and other educational materials are all paid for by the state, the students merely making a small contribution to buy certain materials for independent study.

# RELIGION

Freedom of religious belief is a basic, long-standing policy of the Chinese government. The Constitution of the People's Republic of China clearly stipulates: Citizens of the People's Republic of China enjoy freedom of religious belief. No state organ, public organization or individual may compel citizens to believe in, or not to believe in, any religion; nor may they discriminate against citizens who believe in, or do not believe in, any religion. The state protects normal religious activities. No one may make use of religion to engage in activities that disrupt public order, impair the health of citizens or interfere with the educational system of the state. Religious bodies and religious affairs are not subject to any foreign domination.

This freedom includes recognizing all religious groups' right to exist as well as their right to carry out normal religious activities. It also includes the recognition that all religious groups are equal in the eyes of the Chinese government and that none occupies a privileged position.

Within the limits prescribed by the Constitution, each religious group, in accordance with the principles of independence, self-government and self-administration of its places of worship, is free to carry out religious functions, establish places of worship and religious schools according to its actual needs, publish religious books and periodicals and print and distribute religious scriptures. Religious organizations and their followers can hold religious services in their places of worship or, according to custom, in the worshippers' own homes.

At present, the major religious faiths in China are Buddhism, Islam, Protestantism, Catholicism and Taoism. Each faith has its own religious organizations: the Chinese Buddhist Association, the Chinese Islamic Association, the Three-Self Patriotic Movement Committee of the Protestant Churches of China, the Chinese Patriotic Catholic Association and the Chinese Taoist Association. Besides these, there are also local religious associations.

It is generally believed that Buddhism first came to China in 67 A.D. during the reign of Emperor Ming Di of the Eastern Han dynasty, but the official records hold that it was first propagated in China in 2 B.C. during the reign of Emperor Ai Di of the Western Han dynasty. Afterwards, because it was sanctioned by many of the successive dynasties Buddhism became widespread and had a tremendous impact on the development of Chinese thought, culture and art. Lamaism is a Buddhist sect which flourishes in the regions inhabited by the Tibetan and Mongolian nationalities. The Gelu Sect (also known as the Yellow Sect) is an offshoot of Lamaism which first emerged in the early 15th century as a product of the long-term interaction of Buddhism with the native Tibetan religion.

Islam first reached China about the middle of the 7th century. As commercial and cultural contacts between East and West developed, Arab and Persian traders began calling on China in increasing numbers and they spread the teachings of Mohammed during their

A Newly Opened Mosque on Ox Street in Beijing

visits. Thus the Islamic faith has been practiced in China for more than 1,300 years, and still has a large following among ten of China's minority nationalities — the Hui, Uygur, Kazak, Uzbek, Tajik, Tatar, Kirgiz, Dongxiang, Salar and Bonan. These peoples reside largely in the provinces and autonomous regions of Xinjiang, Ningxia, Gansu, Qinghai, Henan and Yunnan.

Christianity in China most often refers to Protestantism, the introduction of which dates back to China's defeat in the Opium War and the subsequent signing of the Treaty of Nanjing in 1842. Among the concessions which the Western powers forced on the Qing

Taoists at the White Cloud Temple in Beijing

government with this unequal treaty was the right of Western missionaries to proselytize in China. Thus from the very first day that Protestantism entered China. it took on the color of colonialism. In 1950, Chinese Christians launched the Three-Self Patriotic Movement (self-administration, self-support and self-propagation). In 1954, the Three-Self Patriotic Movement Committee of the Protestant Churches of China was founded, enabling Chinese Protestants to break away from Western control and establish an organization representative of the broad masses of Chinese Protestants. At present, this organization has more than 700,000 members.

Although Catholicism was first brought to China more than 300 years ago by Jesuit missionaries, it did not gain sizable numbers of adherents until one hundred years ago when Catholic missionaries received the backing of the forces of foreign imperialism which were then encroaching upon Chinese sovereignty. In 1950, Chinese Catholics throughout the country launched an anti-imperialist movement and formed local patriotic organizations — the Chinese Patriotic Catholic Associations. In 1956, the Preparatory Committee for the Chinese Patriotic Catholic Association was formed, and in 1957 the association was formally established in Beijing.

Taoism sprang directly from the Han nationality and is an indigenous religion of China. Characterized by a positive attitude towards the occult and the metaphysical, Taoism takes Lao Zi, the 6th century B.C. Chinese philosopher and mystic, as its sage and his *Dao De Jing* as its canon. Taoism derives directly from the ancient Han Chinese tradition of spirit worship and necromancy, and its adherents believe that by following a certain regimen (including meditation and ascetic practices) they can attain a state bordering on immortality. In 1957, the Chinese Taoist Association was established with the aim of bring-

Christians Celebrating Christmas Eve at a Catholic Church

ing together all Taoists and Taoist scholars in China to study the history and the doctrines of this religion.

During the ten years of havoc wrought by Lin Biao and the Gang of Four in the "cultural revolution", all religious organizations in China were laid to waste. However, after 1976 the Chinese government not only restored freedom of religious belief but also took measures to repair the damage which had been wrought during that period.

At present, the majority of national and local religious organizations have resumed their activities and the clergy of each religious faith have once again taken up their clerical activities and religious duties. As a token of the great im-portance it attaches to religion, in the past few years the government has embarked on a project to restore and reopen large numbers of temples and churches which had fallen into disrepair. These include several dozen major religious edifices, including China's most ancient Buddhist temple, the Baima (White Horse) Temple in Luoyang, as well as the Huajue Mosque in Xi'an, the Protestant Mu'en Church in Shanghai, the Shishi (Stone Chamber) Catholic Cathedral in Guangzhou, the Dazhao Temple in Tibet, and China's largest Lamaist temple, the Labuleng Temple in Gansu.

At present, friendly contacts between religious organizations in China and the rest of the world are increasing daily.

111

# A BRIEF OUTLINE OF CHINESE HISTORY

China is one of the cradles of world civilization; it has an extremely rich cultural heritage and nearly 4,000 years of recorded history.

Approximately 4,000 years ago Chinese society entered a period of slave society which lasted throughout the Xia dynasty (c. 21st-16th centuries B.C.), Shang dynasty (c. 16th century B.C.-1066 B.C.), Western Zhou dynasty (c. 1066-771 B.C.) and Spring and Autumn period (770-476 B.C.). From the Spring and Autumn period through the Warring States period (475-221 B.C.) of the Eastern Zhou dynasty (770-221 B.C.) China underwent a period of violent social upheaval, resulting in the gradual evolution from a slave society into a feudal society. It was during this time that some of the greatest philosophers in Chinese history lived: Confucius, Mencius, Mozi, Laozi, Zhuangzi, Shang Yang and Han Fei. The great poet Qu Yuan, the author of the *Li Sao,* was also active during this period.

In 221 B.C., Qin Shi Huang, the First Emperor of the Qin dynasty, brought the Warring States period to a close when he established the first centralized monarchy in Chinese history and extended his rule over numerous ethnic groups.

It was not until the Han dynasty (206 B.C.-220 A.D.) that the rule of the landlord-dominated centralized feudal monarchy was firmly established in China. During the Han period, agriculture and the handicraft industry made rapid development, commerce flourished, and there were a variety of notable achievements in culture and science, including Sima Qian's *The Records of the Historians,* China's first comprehensive historical work, and the seismograph invented by Zhang Heng. In addition, the invention of paper, perhaps China's greatest contribution to world culture, was also a product of this period.

With the overthrow of the Han dynasty, China entered the Three Kingdoms period (220-280), in which Chinese territory was divided between the states of Wei, Shu Han and Wu. At the end of this period, China was briefly united again during the Jin dynasty (265-420), but this was followed by a period of division during the Northern and Southern dynasties (480-581). The Sui dynasty (581-618) and Tang dynasty (618-907) which followed ushered in a period of national unity which witnessed the rapid development of China's feudal society and the increasing bondage of the peasants to the land. The Tang dynasty was a period of particularly vigorous commercial development. Among the outstanding achievements of this period were the calculation of the relation of the circle's circumference to its diameter by Zu Chongzhi of the Northern and Southern dynasties; the design and construction of the Zhaozhou Bridge, the world's oldest stone arc bridge, by Li Chun in the Sui dynasty; and the earliest determination of the earth's meridian lines by the Tang dynasty monk Yi Xing. Gunpowder, invented in China at an early date, was still not being used by the Chinese for military purposes at the time of the Tang dynasty. In the field of literature, the Tang dynasty produced a number of brilliant poets such as Li Bai, Du Fu and Bai Juyi.

When the Tang dynasty came to an end in 907, China underwent a period of disunity called the Five Dynasties (907-960), which was followed by the Liao (907-1125), Song (960-1279), Western Xia (1032-1227) and Jin (1115-1234) dynasties, their reigns overlapping as they ruled different parts of the country. Altogether, China underwent 460 years of disunity before finally being fully reunited again under the Mongols during the Yuan dynasty in 1271.

This 460-year period also yielded numerous outstanding achievements in the fields of science, literature and technology. The process of printing with movable type letters was invented by Bi Sheng, enabling China to take a great step forward in the field of book publishing. The compass, which had been invented by the Chinese at a much earlier date, was used in navigation as early as the 11th century. At this time, Song poetry and Yuan dynasty drama were newly emergent art forms. The famous literary artists of this period include the poets Su Dongpo and Li Qingzhao, and the dramatist Guan Hanqing. Commerce and international trade also developed rapidly

# A SIMPLE CHRONOLOGY OF CHINESE HISTORY

| | |
|---|---|
| Xia dynasty | c. 21st-16th centuries B.C. |
| Shang dynasty | c. 16th-11th centuries B.C. |
| Western Zhou dynasty | c. 11th century B.C.-770 B.C. |
| Eastern Zhou dynasty | |
| Spring and Autumn period | 770-476 B.C. |
| Warring States period | 475-221 B.C. |
| Qin dynasty | 221-207 B.C. |
| Western Han dynasty | 206 B.C.-24 A.D. |
| Eastern Han dynasty | 25-220 |
| Three Kingdoms (Wei, Shu Han, Wu) | 220-265 |
| Western Jin dynasty | 265-316 |
| Eastern Jin dynasty | 317-420 |
| Northern and Southern dynasties | 420-589 |
| Sui dynasty | 581-618 |
| Tang dynasty | 618-907 |
| Five Dynasties | 907-960 |
| Liao dynasty | 916-1125 |
| Northern Song dynasty | 960-1127 |
| Southern Song dynasty | 1127-1279 |
| Western Xia dynasty | 1032-1227 |
| Jin dynasty | 1115-1234 |
| Yuan dynasty | 1271-1368 |
| Ming dynasty | 1368-1644 |
| Qing dynasty | 1644-1911 |
| Republic of China | 1912-1949 |
| People's Republic of China | Established in 1949 |

during the Song dynasty, and the Venetian Marco Polo made his famed journey during the Yuan dynasty.

The Yuan dynasty was followed by the Ming (1368-1644) and Qing (1644-1911) dynasties, during which the feudal period in China gradually drew to a close, the seeds of capitalism having already been sown by the late Ming dynasty. Under Ming and Qing rule, China was a united multi-ethnic country. The great Ming physician Li Shizhen compiled and published his famous medical treatise *Compendium of Materia Medica* which was later translated into many foreign languages and disseminated widely throughout the world. The Ming scientist Song Yingxing wrote the renowned *Exposition on the Works of Nature,* a work reflecting this period's high level of scientific achievements. The novel *A Dream of Red Mansions* by Cao Xueqin, one of the greatest masterpieces in all of Chinese literature, is also a product of this period.

Since ancient times, China has engaged in friendly contacts with the people of foreign countries. The Han dynasty Imperial Emissary Zhang Qian was dispatched on diplomatic expeditions to what is now northern Afghanistan and in the process opened China's famed Silk Road. The Tang monk Xuan Zang journeyed throughout Central Asia and India to gather Buddhist scriptures and left descriptions of the places he visited in his 12-volume *Records of Western Travels.* In the Ming dynasty, Zheng He, an envoy of the Emperors Chengzu and Xuanzong, made a total of seven sailing expeditions which took him as far as the coast of East Africa.

Throughout the imperial period, Chinese society frequently erupted in peasant uprisings. The earliest of these was the Chen Sheng-Wu Guang Uprising (209 B.C.) at the close of the Qin dynasty. This was followed by the Yellow Turban Uprising at the end of the Han dynasty, the great peasant rebellion led by Huang Chao at the close of the Tang dynasty, and the peasant revolt led by Li Zicheng at the end of the Ming dynasty.

These peasant uprisings dealt devastating blows at the landlord class and paved the way for the social revolutions which were to follow. The Opium War of 1840 was one of the greatest turning points in Chinese history, and led to China being gradually reduced to the state of semi-feudal, semicolonial society. From the middle of the 19th century, the Chinese people launched numerous revolutionary movements to oppose the rule of imperialism and colonialism, including the largest peasant uprisings in Chinese history, the Taiping Revolution (1851-1864) and the Revolution of 1911 led by Dr. Sun Yat-sen, both of which met with failure. However, beginning from the establishment of the Chinese Communist Party in 1921, the Chinese people waged 28 years of bitter, protracted struggle and underwent untold suffering and hardships before finally overthrowing the rule of imperialism, feudalism and bureaucratic capitalism, and establishing the People's Republic of China in 1949.

## THE INVENTION OF PAPER

In the early days, the Chinese discovered that washing silk floss on a bamboo mat left a thin layer of sediment, which, as it dried, coagulated to form a thin flexible sheet which could be used to write on or to wrap things. As this paper was made from silk residues, it was too expensive to be manufactured on a large scale and put into general use. However, with the use of linen manufacturing, people began to make paper from linen scraps as well, first pounding them to a pulp, which was then boiled and spread out to dry on sheets. Through the process of constant practice and experimentation, the technique of making paper from plant fiber-based fabrics was gradually perfected in the Western Han dynasty (206 B.C.-24 A.D.).

In 105, a new paper making process was discovered by Cai Lun, which made possible the manufacture of a finer grade of paper. According to his method, bark, linen scraps and old fishnets were pounded to a pulp and spread out on colander to drain off the water. When it dried, this pulp formed a kind of paper which was named "Cailun", after the name of the man who invented it. The use of this paper spread rapidly across China and then on to its neighboring countries. Between the third and fourth centuries, Cailun paper was introduced to Viet Nam and Korea, in the seventh century to Japan and in the eighth century to the Middle East before finally reaching Europe in the 12th century.

# MAO ZEDONG AND MAO ZEDONG THOUGHT

Mao Zedong was one of the founders of the Chinese Communist Party, and for nearly half a century remained the chief leader of the People's Liberation Army and the People's Republic of China. Though he committed serious "left" errors in his later years, his indelible, meritorious service in founding and building up the Chinese Party, army and state, his irreplaceable contributions to gaining China's freedom, independence and sovereignty, his unwavering sympathy and support for the cause of the oppressed people throughout the world won him the deepest love and respect of the Chinese people and made him a great Marxist, an outstanding proletarian revolutionary, as well as a strategist, theorist and internationalist. Unquestionably he will go down in history as one of the greatest figures of the 20th century.

In the 1920s and 1930s, the newly-established CPC suffered heavily right and "left" deviations, misinterpreting Marxism. Such erroneous tendency among some of the Party leaders caused the CPC to lose virtually all of its urban organizations and over 90 percent of its rural bases to the KMT, and brought the Chinese revolution to the brink of total failure. With his profound understanding of the conditions within Chinese society and the theories of Marxism-Leninism, as well as his deep political insight, Mao Zedong waged a long hard struggle against these tendencies. He believed that the study of Marxism-Leninism was by no means mere "book worship", but the actual apprehension of its viewpoint, its methods and its essential principles. He advocated that to lead the Chinese revolution to victory, the Chinese Communist Party must proceed from actual Chinese social conditions and integrate the essential principles of Marxism-Leninism with concrete Chinese practices. It was in the process of combating dogmatism and summing up the CPC's historical experience that Mao Zedong Thought took shape and developed.

Prior to the founding of New China in 1949, Mao Zedong

enriched the Marxist-Leninist theory of the leadership of the proletariat in the democratic revolution with his theory of the new democratic revolution, which targeted itself against imperialism, feudalism and bureaucrat-capitalism on the basis of the worker-peasant alliance under the leadership of the proletariat.

China's bourgeoisie, as Mao had discovered, consisted of two sectors, the big bourgeoisie (the comprador or bureaucrat bourgeoisie) which was dependent on imperialism; and the national bourgeoisie which, though exploiting the people, was smothered by competition from both the imperialist powers and the big bourgeoisie, and unlike the former had revolutionary potential. Thus for the first time in Communist history, Mao suggested that the Chinese proletariat should endeavor to obtain the participation of the national bourgeoisie in the united front under the proletarian leadership, and in special circumstances even include part of the big bourgeoisie in order to isolate the main target to the greatest extent.

Mao also discovered that in a feudal country like China, there was no bourgeois democracy as in the West, and the reactionary ruling classes enforced their dictatorship over the people by armed force. Therefore he held that the Chinese revolution could not but take the form of a protracted armed struggle. Furthermore, based on the fact that China was an agricultural country, he proposed that the peasants were the most reliable ally of the proletariat and the main force of the revolution under its leadership.

In his own words, "the united front and armed struggle are the two basic weapons for defeating the enemy". Together with Party building, they constituted the "three magic weapons" of the Chinese revolution which ensured its final victory.

After the founding of the People's Republic, instead of an abrupt confiscation of the private means of production owned by the bourgeoisie and capitalists as took place in the Soviet Union, the CPC under Mao's leadership took concrete steps for a gradual socialist transformation of the means of production, such as effecting policies of redemption and joint state-private ownership, while carrying out socialist industrialization on a large scale. Furthermore, by combining the concepts of people's democracy

and dictatorship over the reactionaries, Mao created the theory of the people's democratic dictatorship, thus further enriching the Marxist-Leninist theory of the dictatorship of the proletariat.

With the establishment of the socialist system in China, a number of contradictions arose among the people who share the same fundamental interests. To solve these contradictions and deal with other social changes which were taking place, Mao proposed the policy of "unity — criticism — unity" to proceed from a unity of goodwill, and through criticism, self-criticism and an exchange of views, reach a common understanding and achieve the final goal of unity. In handling the Communist Party's relations with other democratic parties, Mao elaborated the policy of "long-term co-existence and mutual supervision" and that of "let a hundred flowers blossom and a hundred schools of thought contend" in both science and culture. In the economic sphere, he stressed an overall consideration for the interests of the state, collective and individual, and proceeding from China's actual socio-economic conditions, acknowledged the necessity for the co-existence of state, collective and private sectors in China's economy.

Mao Zedong also enriched Marxism-Leninism through his theories on the building of the revolutionary army and military strategy; on policy and tactics; on ideological, political and cultural work; and on Party building. Mao's thought can be reduced to three basic points: seeking truth from facts, the mass line and independence. Seeking truth from facts means proceeding from reality, combining theory with practices, and opposing the subjective and dogmatic study and practice of Marxism-Leninism isolated from the realities of Chinese society and revolution. By the mass line, he meant that everything should be for the masses, and that the masses should be relied upon in everything; in his own words, "from the masses, to the masses". Independence means that China should rely mainly on its own strength and find its own road to progress in accordance with its own conditions. It also means that the road to revolution and construction which suits the characteristics of a country must be explored, and followed by its own people, and that no other nation has the right to impose its views.

For nearly 50 years, Mao Zedong Thought, which in actuality represents the collective wisdom of Mao Zedong and his close comrades, has remained the major political and theoretical guide to action for the CPC and proved itself to be the most beneficial and effective theory in leading the Chinese revolution to victory. It remains the most valuable spiritual asset of the CPC. However, since the third session of the 11th CPC National Congress, the Party leadership has realized that it is entirely wrong to adopt a dogmatic attitude towards the sayings of Mao Zedong, to regard whatever he said as immutable truth, and to be unwilling to admit honestly that he made mistakes in his later years during the "cultural revolution"; on the other hand, it is incorrect to negate the scientific value of Mao Zedong Thought and deny its guiding role in China's revolution and construction simply because of these mistakes. A distinction has been made between the scientific system of Mao Zedong Thought and Mao's mistakes in his later years. Enbodying all of the positive experience gained in the course of integrating the universal principles of Marxism-Leninism with the concrete practice of China's revolution and construction over half a century, Mao Zedong Thought will continue to guide China's political life for a long time to come.

# THE LONG MARCH

After Chiang Kai-shek betrayed the Kuomintang-Communist cooperation in 1927 and staged a coup d'etat in which thousands of revolutionaries were massacred, the urban Party organization was practically wiped out. In response, the Communist Party expanded its revolutionary bases in various parts of the countryside, fighting regular battles and using guerrilla tactics at the same time. A central base area was established in Jiangxi Province with a provisional central government in Ruijin.

To "kill the baby in its cradle", Chiang Kai-shek amassed some 100,000 troops and launched one "encirclement and suppression" campaign after another against the central base area. The Communist Party won the first four campaigns but suffered heavy losses in the fifth, which took place in 1934 due to a recklessly adventurist policy which was being pursued by the then Party leadership. Facing the danger of total annihilation, the Party decided to evacuate and try to establish a new revolutionary base.

However, the main Red Army forces withdrew in great disorder. Pursued from behind, blocked in front and pounded from the air, they lost more than half of their men within three months. At this juncture, Mao Zedong advised the Red Army to move into the southwestern province of Guizhou, away from Chiang Kai-shek's main forces. In early 1935, after the Red Army captured the city of Zunyi in northern Guizhou, an enlarged meeting of the Political Bureau of the Party was held there. Mao Zedong criticized the mistaken military strategy; Zhou Enlai, Zhu De and others supported his position. The meeting reorganized the central committee and set up a military command group with Mao Zedong as chairman.

By the end of January, 1935, the Red Army was on the move again. Through clever maneuvering, the Red Army broke through Chiang Kai-

The Long-Marchers Climbing the Snow-Covered Mount Jiajin in Sichuan

The Long Marchers not only withstood extreme hardship for constant lack of food and shelter, but very often they had to elude or fight back against numerically superior Kuomintang troops or break through encirclements by the armies of provincial warlords sent to interrupt them. The 12,500-kilometer long trek witnessed numerous heroic deeds on the part of its participants, giving hope to Chinese progressives everywhere that these revolutionaries would eventually play an important role in the liberation of China.

shek's encirclement and opened the way towards northwest China. This marked the beginning of the famous Long March. The rationale for the move was to fight the Japanese aggressors in the north and save the nation.

In a year's time, the fighters passed through 11 provinces on foot crossing over some of the most harsh and forbidding terrain in China. They crossed 24 dangerous rivers and 18 mountain ranges, five of which were snow-capped all year round.

In October 1935, the First Front Army entered northern Shaanxi Province. A year later, the Second and Fourth Front armies arrived via different routes and joined forces with the First Front Army. Only one-tenth of the original army and Party personnel (about 30,000) who had set out reached Shaanxi. The rest had either died or stayed behind as guerrilla fighters. The epic Long March was thus triumphantly concluded. From then on, Yan'an in northern Shaanxi became the center of revolution throughout the rest of the war against Japanese aggression.

# THE LUNISOLAR CALENDAR

The lunisolar calendar appeared very early in Chinese history. A written calendar was in use as early as the late Zhou (770-221 B.C.) and the early Han (206 B.C.-23 A.D.) dynasties.

Like other calendars, the lunisolar calendar divides the year into days and months. Before China's 1911 Revolution, with the sole exception of the celestial calendar promulgated by the Taiping Heavenly Kingdom (1851-1864), all other Chinese calendars were based on the lunisolar calendar.

The divisions of the calendar are based on the waxing and waning of the moon while taking into consideration the summer and winter solar terms. In the lunisolar calendar, the length of the year and months is determined by various celestial phenomena.

The lunisolar calendar is superior to the lunar calendar, its only defect being the large difference between the length of the ordinary years and leap years.

Since the founding of the People's Republic in 1949, the Gregorian calendar has been adopted as China's official calendar. The lunisolar calendar, however, is still used to mark traditional festivals and historical occasions, and by peasants to observe farming seasons.

## THE COUNTRY WITH THE LARGEST VARIETY OF BIRDS IN THE WORLD

According to a survey undertaken in 1982, of the 8,616 to 9,021 kinds of birds which exist in the world today, 1,183, or 13 percent of the total number, can be found in China, making it the country with the largest variety of birds in the world. A survey conducted in 1983 discovered an additional four kinds of birds which had been overlooked a year earlier.

# THE 24 TERMS OF THE TRADITIONAL CHINESE SOLAR CALENDAR

In ancient times, China's solar terms sometimes referred to a period of time. For example, the period during which the sun passed through the portion of the ecliptic (the apparent path of the sun among the stars) from 0 to 15 degrees was referred to as the Spring Equinox (the fourth solar term). At present, however, the solar terms all refer to specific days, the 0 degree point on the ecliptic marking the Spring Equinox and the 15 degree point denoting the term called the Pure Brightness (Qingming). The Pure Brightness Festival is celebrated in China and throughout East Asia.

According to this system, the entire year is divided into 24 portions based on the sun's position on the ecliptic. Beginning with the solar term called the Small Cold, each 15 degree movement of the sun along the ecliptic represents one solar term. The first day of each solar term is referred to by the name of the term.

By the Spring and Autumn period (770-476 B.C.), the four solar terms, the Spring Equinox, the Summer Solstice, the Autumn Equinox and the Winter Solstice, had already been accurately calculated. In the ensuing centuries, with the steady progress in agricultural production, the solar calendar was gradually perfected. By the time of the Qin and Han dynasties (221 B.C.-220 A.D.), all 24 solar terms had been computed, and served as the major guideline for all agricultural activities.

The Ancient Imperial Observatory

# CHART OF THE 24 SOLAR TERMS

| | | |
|---|---|---|
| Spring | 1. Beginning of Spring | February 4 or 5 |
| | 2. Rain Water | February 19 or 20 |
| | 3. Waking of Insects | March 5 or 6 |
| | 4. Spring Equinox | March 20 or 21 |
| | 5. Pure Brightness | April 4 or 5 |
| | 6. Grain Rain | April 20 or 21 |
| Summer | 7. Beginning of Summer | May 5 or 6 |
| | 8. Grain Full | May 21 or 22 |
| | 9. Grain in Ear | June 5 or 6 |
| | 10. Summer Solstice | June 21 or 22 |
| | 11. Slight Heat | July 7 or 8 |
| | 12. Great Heat | July 23 or 24 |
| Autumn | 13. Beginning of Autumn | August 7 or 8 |
| | 14. Limit of Heat | August 23 or 24 |
| | 15. White Dew | September 7 or 8 |
| | 16. Autumnal Equinox | September 23 or 24 |
| | 17. Cold Dew | October 8 or 9 |
| | 18. Frost's Descent | October 23 or 24 |
| Winter | 19. Beginning of Winter | November 7 or 8 |
| | 20. Slight Snow | November 22 or 23 |
| | 21. Great Snow | December 7 or 8 |
| | 22. Winter Solstice | December 21 or 22 |
| | 23. Slight Cold | January 5 or 6 |
| | 24. Great Cold | January 20 or 21 |

# THE HEAVENLY STEMS AND EARTHLY BRANCHES

The "Heavenly Stems" is the general name for the "Ten Stems" which are frequently used as symbols to denote numerical order: 甲 (jia), 乙 (yi), 丙 (bing), 丁 (ding), 戊 (wu), 己 (ji), 庚 (geng), 辛 (xin), 壬 (ren), 癸 (gui).

The "Earthly Branches" is the general name for "Twelve Branches", which in ancient times were used to record chronological order: 子 (zi), 丑 (chou), 寅 (yin), 卯 (mao), 辰 (chen), 巳 (si), 午 (wu), 未 (wei), 申 (shen), 酉 (you), 戌 (xu), 亥 (hai).

The "Stems and Branches" refers to the counting system wherein one character from each of the two series is combined to form a regular sequence composed of 60 paired combinations. The sequence thus formed was used in ancient times as a revolving cycle to denote the years, months, days and hours.

This system has survived in the present-day lunar calendar, which still uses the Heavenly Stems and Earthly Branches to enumerate the years and days. In Chinese history, the Stems and Branches were used to refer to events occurring in certain years. For example, the Revolution of 1911 is known as the "辛亥 (xin hai)" Revolution in all Chinese writings.

## THE WORLD'S FIRST HEAT BALLOON

Sometime between 907 and 960, a Chinese woman named Xin Qi constructed a heat balloon out of thin bamboo strips which was launched by means of a basket containing burning rosin suspended at the bottom. After its invention, the Chinese used the balloon to convey military signals. It was the world's first heat balloon.

# PRESERVING CHINA'S HISTORICAL SITES

China's historical sites, national treasures which have been bequeathed to the present-day citizens of the People's Republic by their ancestors, are not only one of the great symbols of Chinese civilization, but also inestimably precious material for all those who wish to study and better appreciate China's cultural heritage. For these reasons, the government of the People's Republic attaches great importance to the work of preserving the nation's historical monuments and artifacts.

Shortly after the founding of the People's Republic in 1949, the Central Government issued a decree banning the export of precious artifacts and art objects, thereby stemming the grave drain of the country's relics which had continued unabated during the previous 100 years.

In 1960, the State Council adopted a number of provisional regulations concerning the preservation of the nation's historical monuments and relics. These regulations stipulate that "within the borders of the People's Republic of China, all relics of genuine historic, artistic or scientific interest are under the protection of the state. It is strictly forbidden to damage them or appropriate them for export abroad. The people's governments at all levels are responsible for the preservation of the historical monuments within the areas under their jurisdiction. All relics which at present remain unearthed are national property." These regulations further stipulate the scope of preservation work and the methods to be employed.

In the period from 1961 to 1982, China successively promulgated two lists of historical sites designated for state protection, with a total of 242 items. Those places designated for protection can be subdivided into the following six categories:

1. Revolutionary sites and revolutionary memorials and monuments: 43 in total;

2. Cave temples: 19;

3. Ancient buildings and historical memorial buildings: 105;

4. Carved stones and stone inscriptions: 13;

5. Ancient historical sites: 36; and

6. Ancient graves and tomb sites: 26.

The remaining 43 percent of the items on the two lists are all ancient buildings.

During the decade of the "cultural revolution" (1966-1976) many ancient Chinese monuments and artifacts were seriously damaged in the so-called "Destroy the Four Olds" campaign. Most severely damaged were some ancient tomb sites as well as a number of ancient temples and the Buddhist statues they contained. After the fall of the Gang of Four in 1976, the situation took a considerable turn for the better and most of the damaged monuments and relics are under repair. Some have already been restored to their original form and reopened to tourists.

Article 22 of the Constitution of the People's Republic of China adopted in 1982 stipulates: "It is the nation's policy to protect its historical monuments, its valuable artifacts, and all other objects connected with its cultural and historical heritage."

China's policy of preserving its historical monuments and relics is more than a mere set of regulations, for it includes a variety of measures being taken pursuant to the policy's goals. For example, the Historical Relics Bureau of the Ministry of Culture is now preparing to establish several centers for scientific research in historical preservation to ensure that China's cultural legacy will pass intact into the hands of future generations.

# THE MATHEMATICIAN WHO FIRST PRECISELY CALCULATED THE RATIO OF THE CIRCUMFERENCE OF THE CIRCLE TO ITS DIAMETER

In the mid-5th century the celebrated Chinese mathematician Zu Chongzhi precisely calculated the ratio of the circumference of the circle to its diameter to be $> 3.1415926$ and $< 3.1415927$. He performed the calculation with the aid of the Pythagorean theorem, using numerous uniform-sized bamboo markers as a unit of calculation. Zu Chongzhi performed this feat more than 1,000 years earlier than mathematicians in Europe.

# THE EVOLUTION OF CHINESE COSTUME

Chinese costume has an age-old history and is characterized by its exquisite workmanship, brilliant colors and strong national character. Chinese costume has a recorded history of more than 5,000 years. Despite the numerous changes in fashion which have occurred during this period, Chinese costume can be divided into two main styles: two-piece suits comprised of a coat and a pair of trousers, and robes in a variety of styles.

Previous to the Zhou dynasty (c. 1066-771 B.C.), Chinese costume consisted basically of a two-piece suit made up of an *yi* (tunic) and a *shang* (a kind of kilt). Many styles of clothing which developed in later periods, such as the *hufu* (non-Han garment), the *kuzhe* (trousers and robe) and the woman's *ruqun* (short jacket and skirt), were patterned on this earlier two-piece suit. Like primitive Chinese written characters, the designs printed on these garments were simple but rich with symbolic meaning.

After the Zhou dynasty, the patterns printed on the garments were designed such that the upper and lower portions of the garments matched neatly and the right and left sides were symmetrical.

Robes first appeared in China during the late Spring and Autumn period and early Warring States period (c. 475-221 B.C.). Known as the *shenyi* (long coat), this style developed into the *pao* of later ages. In the *shenyi,* the shirt and skirt were joined into a single garment for

### THE EVOLUTION OF CHINESE WOMEN'S DRESS

Han

Wei

Tang

Song

the first time, the men's version resembling a short kilt and the women's a long dress.

Later, Chinese costume became increasingly complex and became an indication of the wearer's social status. Some classes wore tunics and capes, some wore narrow-waisted short-sleeved garments which exposed the chest and others wore narrow-sleeved, broad-collared long gowns which reached the ground and were bound at the waist by a hanging sash. During this period, women generally wore a short tunic and a skirt.

The costumes of the Three Kingdoms period (220-280) and the Northern and Southern dynasties (420-581) carried forward the style of the Han dynasty, becoming both more practical in design and more ornamented. After the year of 420 A.D. the civil strife at this time prompted massive migration from the north to the central plains along the Huanghe River valley, and the new inhabitants of this area brought with them the light and convenient styles of dress worn by the non-Han tribes of the north. Two originally non-Han garments adopted during this period were the *kuzhe* (trousers and robe) and *liangdang* (a vest-like garment.)

During the Sui and Tang dynasties (581-907), the long robe became increasingly popular. The vigorous economic and cultural development of the Tang dynasty ushered in a period of new sartorial refinement. The most common garments of this period were *tan xiong* (a garment which revealed the chest), the long skirt, the loose tunic, the narrow-sleeved tunic and a kind of tunic bound at the waist with a sash. The dress code at this time was both stringent and specific. With the burgeoning of China's foreign trade in the Tang dynasty, Chinese garments and silk were increasingly exported abroad.

An outstanding characteristic of the costumes of the Tang and Song dynasties (618-1279) is the vertical and horizontal symmetry of their designs.

Song dynasty (960-1279) costumes carried forward the principles of style and design prevalent during the Tang period, but the range of colors used in women's garments increased greatly.

The costumes of the Yuan dynasty (1271-1368) adopted a number of design features characteristic of the garments of the non-Han minority peoples, such as round-collared and collarless garments.

Yuan

Ming

Qing

*Shenyi*

*Kuzhe*
(trousers and robe of Northern
and Southern dynasties)

Typical Woman's Dress of Tang, Ming and Qing Dynasties

The Ming and Qing dynasties witnessed a period of rapid development in Chinese costume design. The costumes of the upper classes became more exquisite and colorful and fine embroidery work was used as decoration. Realism was stressed in these designs, which often featured bunches of flowers and swarms of butterflies rendered in meticulous detail.

In the early 20th century, the long robe, the tunic and the sheath dress with a slit skirt became increasingly fashionable. After the Revolution of 1911, Sun Yat-sen took the lead in reforming Chinese dress by having a clothing designer consolidate the tight collars and loose waists of Chinese garments and create a simple and utilitarian Chinese tunic suit. This suit, known in Chinese as the Zhongshan suit after Sun Yat-sen, has retained its popularity down to the present day and is worn as both formal and everyday attire by Chinese men. Mao Zedong wore such a tunic suit when he proclaimed the founding of the People's Republic at Tian'anmen in 1949.

Cheongsam, a Time-Honored Chinese Women's Dress

Since 1949, Chinese women's wear has consisted mostly of Lenin suits (similar to tunic suits), light jackets and skirts of various styles, dresses, Western suits and nylon parkas. The cheongsam or *qipao*, a close-fitting women's sheath dress with a high neck and a slit skirt, has also retained its popularity with Chinese women. This elegant garment has had a considerable influence on foreign fashion designs.

# TEA

A cup of strong fragrant tea can quench the thirst, refresh the spirits and aid digestion. This is because it contains caffeine, pigmentation, aromatic oils, vitamins, minerals and protein. Caffeine is tea's most important constituent: slightly bitter in flavor, it can stimulate the central nervous system, clear the mind, increase the elasticity of the muscles, and act as a cardiac stimulant and diuretic. It can reduce the harmful effects of morphine, nicotine and alcohol. Therefore, a cup of strong tea taken after smoking or drinking will be beneficial to the health.

Tea was first cultivated in China some 4,700 years ago. In ancient China, it was used not only as a beverage, but also as a medicinal drug, a garnish for food and a sacrificial offering. During the earliest period of its cultivation, tea was first grown in the region of present-day Sichuan Province. By the Tang dynasty (618-907) tea cultivation had already expanded as far as the Changjiang River, Zhujiang River and Minjiang River basins, forming the basis of what are today's three main Chinese tea-growing regions. By the Tang dynasty, tea drinking had already spread throughout the entire country. Chinese teas are famous throughout the world for their unique color, fragrance, flavor and finely shaped leaves. The *Classics on Tea*, by the Tang dynasty scholar Lu Yu, is the world's earliest treatise on the subject.

The number of varieties of Chinese tea is so great that they have been likened to the stars on a summer night. Among them are eleven kinds which are especially renowned: Pilochun, Lungching, Lu Shan Yun Wu, Chuen-Shan Silver Needle, Fonghwang Tan-Chung, Keemun (Black), Oolong, Houkui, Shih Ting, Pu-Erh or Pu'er and Jasmine Tea.

Tea has always been one of China's principal traditional exports. As early as the 16th century, the Chinese were already shipping large quantities of tea abroad. From then up till the end of the 19th century, China monopolized the world tea market. In 1886, China exported 134,000 tons of tea, or 90 percent of the world market of that time.

In the 1915 World's Fair organized by the United States to commemorate the opening of the Panama Canal, four varieties of tea exhibited by China won awards: Taiping-Houkui, Nanshan-Baimao, Yunhe-Huiming and Zhuchuan-Gougunao.

On the London market, Keemun (Black) Tea has long been acclaimed as having the "fragrance of spring". In America, Japan and countries of Western Europe, connoisseurs have been unanimous in their praise of Biluochun Tea. One European poet once wrote: "In a delicately fragrant cup of Biluochun Tea I can see the radiant spring scenery of southern China."

Japanese people have an especial liking for Oolong Tea, and because of its health-promoting and weight-reducing properties it is referred to in Japan as "slimming tea", or "good-health tea". Chinese tea has also been referred to as "green gold".

Since 1949, China has reclaimed many abandoned tea plantations and made improvements in old ones still under cultivation. Furthermore, there has also been a vast expansion in tea-growing acreage so that today the figure is as high as 1,647,000 acres.

# PORCELAIN

Porcelain is one of the major inventions of China. Seven or eight thousand years ago during the New Stone Age, the inhabitants of the Huanghe River basin, the cradle of ancient Chinese civilization, began to make earthenware pottery out of clay. Having mastered these techniques, they proceeded to create painted pottery.

The quality of the clay used in ancient earthenware pottery is very fine. Before the vessels were fired, their surfaces were rubbed smooth and the color applied. They were then fired in a kiln at approximately 1,000 degrees Centigrade, which fixed the colors permanently and gave the surfaces a glossy sheen.

The linear motifs painted on earthenware vessels are primarily black, but red and white were also used. In some cases, before the motifs were painted on, a red or white slip was first applied as a background, enabling the designs to stand out more sharply. Ancient painted pottery is characterized by beautiful shapes, compact structure, and simple but lively decorative designs.

By the time of the Shang dynasty (c. 16th-11th centuries B.C.), vitreous glazes had come into use. These glazes were dark in color and were called "black glazes". According to chemical analyses, the black-glazed ceramic ware of this period possesses some of the characteristics of porcelain and is the forerunner of the green and blue porcelain ware of later periods. Thus it has been called "primitive porcelain". Primitive porcelain developed gradually and did not attain a high level of artistic maturity until the Eastern Han dynasty (25-220), when the center of its manufacture was located at Shangyu in Zhejiang Province. The quality of the porcelain ware produced there was extremely fine, with thick and even glazes. Modern analysis reveals the perfect fusion of the body. The degree of absorbency and hardness of the body as well as the fusion of the glazes are all up to the present-day standards.

After the Wei and Jin dynasties (220-420 A.D.), porcelain manufacturing spread north, and production techniques were gradually perfected. The Southern and Northern Dynasties period (420-589) was especially successful in using kaolin to produce brilliant white porcelain ware, representing a great breakthrough in the technology of porcelain manufacture.

The Tang and Song dynasties were a time of rapid development in porcelain manufacture. During the Tang dynasty (618-907), the light green *yue* ware produced in Shaoxing, Zhejiang Province in the south, and the white *xing* ware produced in Neiqiu, Hebei Province in the north were outstanding.

During the Song dynasty (960-1279), there were five ma-

## THE FIRST BOOK ON MILITARY STRATEGY IN THE WORLD

*Sun Wu's Art of War* written by Master Sun in the Warring States period was the first military work ever published in the world. It summarized the fighting experience of the new landlord class in their struggle against the declining slaveowning class in the early stage of China's social transformation from a slavery system to feudalism, giving careful and detailed consideration to each aspect of war and expounding incisively on the nature of war in general. It had great influence on later developments in military affairs and philosophy and provides us with very valuable material for the study of pre-Qin history.

The book put forth a number of stategies which have been influential in the formation of the guerrilla approach to warfare, stressing the use of espionage and psychological warfare tactics. Sun Wu's line, "Know the enemy as you know yourself and one hundred battles will bring one hundred victories" was first written in this vein and has a decidedly modern ring to it. It also stresses flexibility in battle plans according to the actual situation, and contains a section on the use of ships. Mao Zedong had high regard for this ancient treatise and the Red Army employed a number of its tactics in fighting the Japanese and Kuomintang armies.

Various translations exist in English, French, German, Czech, Russian and Japanese. In recent years, the Sun Wu text has been the subject of serious study and appraisal by Western researchers in military science.

jor kilns, each producing porcelain of a certain characteristic style: white *ding* ware; powdery blue *ru* ware; the "purple mouth and iron foot" (*zikou tiezu*) ware of the *guan* or official kilns, *ge* ware with its crackled surface, and *jun* ware with its color transmutations taking place during firing.

The Ming (1368-1644) and Qing (1644-1911) dynasties witnessed further developments in Chinese pottery. During these dynasties, porcelain production was centered at Jingdezhen in Jiangxi Province, where an abundance of kaolin was found. The lustrous and translucent porcelain manufactured from this clay is highly treasured. Among the most famous types of porcelain produced during the Ming and Qing are famille rose, blue and white *dou cai* (contending colors), sacrificial red, rouge ware and misty blue eggshell porcelain.

In the latter Tang dynasty, China commenced the large-scale export of porcelain, and Chinese wares found ready markets in East Asia, West Asia, the east coast of Africa and eventually Europe and the Americas as well. Throughout the Song, Yuan, Ming and Qing dynasties, as exports of porcelain increased, Chinese techniques for porcelain manufacture were continuously disseminated abroad, thus promoting economic and cultural exchange between China and the rest of the world.

After the middle of the Qing dynasty, China was simultaneously penetrated by foreign colonialism and torn by civil war, causing the porcelain industry to enter a period of drastic decline. Porcelain production continued to languish up till the establishment of the People's Republic of China in 1949, after which numerous ancient kilns were re-established and traditional porcelain-making techniques revived. At present, China's porcelain manufacturing districts can each carry out all of the procedures required to produce porcelain ware, from the initial excavation and selection of raw materials to the final testing of finished goods.

Besides carrying forward China's ancient traditions and techniques of porcelain manufacture, China's major porcelain centers are also continuously developing new types of porcelain ware. These include the blue and white and famille rose of Jingdezhen, the underglaze decorated ware of Liling, the gold luted ware of Tangshan, the crystal glazed ware of Zibo and the transmuted color glazed ware of Zhejiang Province.

# TRADITIONAL CHINESE PAINTING

Chinese painting has both an age-old history and a splendid tradition. With a strong national character, it occupies a unique place in the history of world art. Chinese traditional painting does not rigidly adhere to the convention of central focus perspective or realistic portrayal, but rather gives the painter freedom in terms of artistic conception, structural composition and method of expression so as to better express his subjective feelings. Chinese painting has absorbed aspects of other forms of art. The result is that after long years of development and particularly under the influence of the scholar painters, it has become a composite artistic style integrating poetry, calligraphy, painting and seal-engraving, a form of expression which is entirely unique to China.

In terms of technique, Chinese painting can be divided into two broad categories: paintings minutely executed in a realistic style and those which employ freehand brushwork. Classified according to subject matter, it can be divided into paintings of figures, landscapes, buildings, flowers, birds, animals, insects and fish. The brush techniques so much emphasized in Chinese painting include not only line drawing (*goufa*), but also stylized expressions of shade and texture (*cunfa*), the dotting method (*dianfa*) and the application of color (*ranfa*). Different expressive effects are also achieved by thinning or thickening the pigment or ink and painting with a dry or moist brush, by deliberately leaving blanks in the composition as well as by varying its sparseness and density. Since the sizes and shapes of the blanks in the painting are different, the very absence of content can itself create rhythm and variety. In terms of format, traditional Chinese paintings can be divided into murals, screens, scrolls, albums and fans. Furthermore, they are frequently mounted against exquisite backgrounds so as to enhance their aesthetic effect.

Figure painting reached maturity during the Warring States period (475-221 B.C.). Landscape paintings and flower-and-bird paintings had already appeared by the time of the Sui and Tang dynasties (589-907) and flourished during the period of the Five Dynasties (907-960) and Song dynasty (960-1279). It was at this time that ink and wash paintings came into vogue.

The Yuan dynasty (1206-1368) witnessed a gradual turn towards the freehand style, a trend which continued throughout the Ming and Qing dynasties (1368-1911) up to the present day. The freehand style stresses the spiritual likeness or vitality of the subject over its physical likeness. During its long history Chinese painting was at various times influenced by foreign art. After the third century, for example, Buddhist art from India became popular, and in the 17th and 18th centuries Western missionaries brought with them the meticulous realism of Western painting which had some influence on the painters of the imperial court.

Traditional Chinese painting requires that when executing a painting the artist must "draw inspiration from nature" while simultaneously "drawing on the inner resources of his emotions". It also requires that the artist's emotions be aroused before he paints and that these feelings linger on after the painting is finished.

The materials used in Chinese painting are writing brushes, ink sticks and slabs, and paper and silk, all of which are manufactured in China.

On appreciating Chinese paintings, one should be aware of the different styles characteristic of the various historical periods. During the Tang dynasty, the golden age of Chinese feudal society, the economy boomed and culture flourished. The elegant painting style which emerged during this period reflected the general prosperity prevailing then. Owing to the influence of the Confucian school of idealist philosophy on the ideology of the Song dynasty, the paintings of this period favor abstract, implied meanings rather than direct expressions. Painting techniques matured considerably during the Song dynasty, and unprecedented achievements were attained in the landscape, figure and flower-and-bird genres. This period witnessed the full blossoming of the realistic style.

During the Yuan dynasty, the expressionist school of painting flourished and many

A Painting by the Famous Chinese Painter Xu Beihong

painters indulged in painting solely for their own personal pleasure. These painters took a subjective approach to painting, emphasizing the expression of their feelings and the attainment of a high level of accomplishment in their brushwork instead of the social functions of their works. The literati of the Ming and Qing dynasties also saw painting as vehicle to express their interests and feelings. They painted with a vigorous boldness, caring little for meticulous refinement.

141

# CHINESE SILK

Chinese silk is known throughout the world for its numerous varieties, which include silk fabric, satin, damask, silk gauze, crepe silk, tough silk, raw silk, georgette crepe, velvet, as well as embroidered silk and printed silk. Because of its fine texture and exquisite workmanship, Chinese silk has often been singled out as being among the finest textiles produced in the Far East.

China was the first country in the world to manufacture and use silk. The importance of its place in Chinese culture is evident from the legend that Lei Zu, the wife of the mythical Yellow Emperor (Huang Di), first taught the Chinese people the art of sericulture.

Although this is only a legend, archaeologists have discovered a partially unraveled silk cocoon among the New Stone Age relics unearthed at a site at Xiyin Village, in Shanxi Province.

During the Shang dynasty (c. 16th-11th centuries B.C.) there were already government-sponsored silk production workshops. By the time of the Zhou dynasty (c. 11th century-771 B.C.) the production of silk had spread as far as the Hanshui River, Huaihe River and Changjiang River valleys. At this time, the Chinese were producing splendid silks with subtle designs woven into the fabric as well as silk decorated with colored embroidery. This was soon followed by the invention of silk gauze and brocade silk. By the time of the Spring and Autumn and Warring States periods (770-221 B.C.), silk was being manufactured throughout China. Considerable progress had been made in weaving and dyeing techniques.

During the Tang dynasty (618-907) further advances were made in silk manufacturing, resulting in even more delicate and exquisite products. By the time of the Qing dynasty (1644-1911), silk production greatly increased, and the silk of Zhejiang Province enjoyed an especially high reputation.

Since ancient times, silk has been one of China's traditional exports. Fine Chinese silks were first exported during the Western Han dynasty in the second century B.C. A portion of the exports was shipped to Korea and Japan, but the majority was shipped along the famous caravan route known as the Silk Road, eventually reaching Western Europe.

China's geography and climate are well-suited for the cultivation of mulberry and oak trees (the leaves of these trees being the natural food of two types of silkworms), and China has numerous mulberry and oak sericulture farms.

Traditionally, the principal centers of China's sericulture industry are the plains surrounding Taihu Lake in Jiangsu Province, the Sichuan basin, the Zhujiang River delta and the Liaodong Peninsula. From ancient times, China has been the world's leading producer of silk and silkworm cocoons. However, in the 20th century, in the several decades prior to liberation, the sericulture industry entered a period of drastic decline and the silk production greatly decreased. After the establishment of New China, the silk and sericulture industries were revived and underwent a period of rapid development. At present, facilities for manufacturing silk can be found throughout China, and exports of raw and finished silk have regained first place in the world.

China currently produces several hundred varieties of silk in thousands of colors and designs. These silk products have found ready markets in more than 100 countries and regions in the world.

## THE GREATEST NAVAL EXPEDITIONS IN HISTORY

Admirals Zheng He and Wang Jinghong led 27,800 officers, men and interpreters on a voyage of 62 ships, the biggest of which was 147 meters long, 60 meters wide, and loaded with over a thousand people.

From 1405 to 1433, they made seven voyages through Malaya, India, Persia, Arabia, East Africa, the Red Sea and Mecca, visiting a total of 37 countries.

The expedition led by Zheng He was about 100 years earlier than the Portuguese explorer Vasco da Gama who rounded the Cape of Good Hope, and was a century earlier than Columbus who went with only three ships and a crew of 67 to discover the New World.

The size of the fleet led by Zheng He and its cargo capacity were unheard of in their day.

# ALCOHOLIC BEVERAGES

Chinese alcoholic beverages not only have an age-old history, but are also extremely rich in variety. The two earliest kinds of liquor in China were *yuan jiu* or "ape wine", which was made by a process of natural fermentation, and *naizi jiu,* a form of liquor made from milk, which made its first appearance during the pastoral period. The ancient Chinese chronicle *Intrigues of the Warring States* makes reference to the fondness which the Chinese of ancient times had for wine: "Yi Di made wine and Yu* drank it and relished it." The wine referred to herein was made of rice or millet and called *huang jiu,* or "yellow wine". There are two varieties of Chinese *huang jiu,* a southern variety made from glutinous rice, and a northern variety made from broomcorn millet. The most famous type of southern Chinese *huang jiu* is Shaoxing Wine and its counterpart in the north is Jimo Wine.

White or clear spirits, usually distilled from sorghum or maize, also have a history which dates back more than a thousand years in China. The technique of making white spirits appears to have first originated in Shanxi Province, which pioneered in the production of the earliest form of white spirits, Fenjiu. From there, the technique was disseminated to Shaanxi, where it was manufactured in the form of what is today's celebrated Xifeng Liquor. From there, it was transmitted across the Qinling Mountains to Sichuan, where Laojiao Daqu Liquor was produced. From there, the technique spread to Guizhou, where white spirits began to be manufactured in the form of Maotai, which is perhaps today's best known Chinese liquor.

Chinese grape wine also has a very long history. An often-quoted line of Tang dynasty poetry refers to the delight of sipping "fine wine in a luminous glass".

* Yu was the legendary founder of the Xia dynasty (c. 21st-16th centuries B.C.), the earliest dynasty in Chinese history.

Certain of China's wines and liquors are renowned abroad as well as at home. Among these, some have a history of more than a thousand years, such as Maotai and Wuliangye. Other celebrated liquors include Yanghe Daqu from Jiangsu, Laojiao from Sichuan and the brandy manufactured by the Zhangyu Distillery in Yantai, Shandong Province. The above-mentioned beverages have won awards at both the Southeast Asian and Panamanian exhibitions.

Domestically, Jiafan Liquor from Shaoxing, Zhuyeqing (Green Bamboo Liquor) from Shanxi, Gujinggong Liquor from Anhui, Dongjiu Liquor from Guizhou and Longyan Chengang Liquor from Fujian have long enjoyed a high reputation. In more recent years, Yantai Wine, Henan White Wine, Sichuan Jiannanchun Liquor and Qingdao Beer have become increasingly popular with consumers at home and abroad.

In September 1979, the Third National Wine and Spirit Competition was held at Lüda in Liaoning Province. In the competition, seven kinds of Chinese alcoholic beverages were awarded Gold or Silver Medals, 18 kinds were given superior ratings and 47 others won honorable mention. The 18 beverages which won the highest honors can be subdivided into four main categories: white spirits, grape and fruit wines, yellow rice and millet wines, and beer.

The Eight Award-Winning Brands of Liquor

# EIGHTEEN AWARD-WINNING ALCOHOLIC BEVERAGES

| Name of beverage | Place of origin |
|---|---|
| *White Spirits:* | |
| 1. Maotai | Renhuai, Guizhou |
| 2. Fenjiu | Fenyang, Shanxi |
| 3. Wuliangye | Yibin, Sichuan |
| 4. Jiannanchun | Jinzhu, Sichuan |
| 5. Gulianggong | Boxian, Anhui |
| 6. Yanghe Daqu | Siyang, Jiangsu |
| 7. Dongjiu | Zunyi, Guizhou |
| 8. Luzhou Laojiao | Luzhou, Guizhou |
| | |
| *Grape and Fruit Wines:* | |
| 1. Yantai Red Wine | Yantai, Shandong |
| 2. China Red Wine | Beijing |
| 3. Shacheng White Wine | Shacheng, Hebei |
| 4. Minquan White Wine | Minquan, Henan |
| 5. Yantai Vermouth | Yantai, Shandong |
| 6. Gold Medal Brandy | Yantai, Shandong |
| 7. Zhuyeqing | Fenyang, Shanxi |
| | |
| *Rice and Millet Wines:* | |
| 1. Shaoxing Rice Wine | Shaoxing, Zhejiang |
| 2. Longyan Chengang Wine | Longyan, Fujian |
| | |
| *Beer:* | |
| Qingdao Beer | Qingdao, Shandong |

A Taoist Making Wine in the Ancient Way

## GOLD AND SILVER MEDAL ALCOHOLIC BEVERAGES

Gold Medal Liquors:

|   |   |   |
|---|---|---|
| 1. | Maotai | Renhuai, Guizhou |
| 2. | Wuliangye | Yibin, Sichuan |
| 3. | Gold Medal Brandy | Yantai, Shandong |
| 4. | Jiafan Rice Wine | Shaoxing, Zhejiang |
| 5. | Zhuyeqing | Fenyang, Shanxi |
| 6. | Dry White Wine | Shacheng, Hebei |

Silver Medal Beverage:

Qingdao Beer      Qingdao, Shandong

# CHINESE JADE

For several millennia, the carving of jade articles has been an intrinsic part of Chinese culture, one reason why Chinese jade is renowned throughout the world. The Chinese people's love and use of jade dates back to ancient times. In 1973, a large quantity of carved jade articles was unearthed at Hemudu in Yuyao County, Zhejiang Province. According to scientific analysis, these articles date back to the Stone Age, and are at least 7,000 years old.

Chinese jade appears in nature in a great variety. The Chinese jade carving industry now uses over 30 types of jade and jade-like precious stones. These include nephrite (which itself encompasses white jade, green jade, black jade and jasper), jadeite, lapis lazuli, turquoise, agate and malachite. With the exception of jadeite, which is quarried in Burma, and lapis lazuli, which comes from Afghanistan, all the other precious stones are found within China.

The majority of Chinese jade is used to make jade articles and objects, with small amounts of the finest quality jade being set aside for jewelry manufacture. According to historical records, jade is found in more than 100 different locations in China. Nephrite, the traditional favorite of Chinese artisans, is quarried both in the Fengtian district of Taiwan and in the Xinjiang Uygur Autonomous Region.

# MEDICAL AND HEALTH SERVICES

Old China was a country plagued by poverty, occasional epidemics and extremely backward medical care. The small number of hospitals were almost exclusively concentrated in large urban areas and medical treatment was extremely costly. Throughout China's vast countryside there was an acute shortage of drugs and doctors.

The founding of the People's Republic in 1949 opened broad vistas for the development of medical and health services. Since then, the People's Government has shown a real concern for the health of the people, mobilizing its forces to expand China's health services and develop a hospital system which embraces every corner of the country. Besides reforming and expanding existing hospitals, large numbers of new hospitals and health-care institutions have been built. In the 31-year interval between 1949 and 1980, the number of hospitals in China grew from 2,600 to 65,911, the number of hospital beds increased from 80,000 to 2,017,088, the number of medical research organizations increased from three to 285 and the number of doctors increased from 363,000 to 1,244,000.

China's medical and health work places much stress on the rural areas where over 80 percent of the population lives. Tremendous changes have taken place in the past three decades. According to 1980 statistics, China has 55,500 hospitals below the county level. These hospitals are equipped with 763,114 beds and staffed by some 1.1 million medical personnel. Moreover, every production brigade has its own co-operative hospital or health station. Urban medical organizations and medical units attached to the People's Liberation Army frequently dispatch medical teams to the countryside to treat the inhabitants of remote areas. Besides carrying out therapeutic and preventive medical work, these teams also offer training to local medical personnel to raise the level of their professional expertise.

Free medical care has now been extended to the staff and workers of government offices on various levels, cultural, educational and puolic health institutions, and to employees of state-owned enterprises (including retirees), officers and men of the People's Liberation Army, disabled servicemen and college students. Members of the immediate families of workers and employees in state-owned enterprises receive medical subsidies when they are sick.

When workers or employees are injured at work, they not only receive free medical care (including visits to clinics and hospitalization), the expenses being shared by the government and the enterprise where they work, but also subsidies covering two-thirds of their food costs during hospitalization. Workers suffering from job-related injuries or illness and women workers who are recuperating after childbirth are entitled to receive full pay. Furthermore, China is now in the midst of establishing numerous clinics and sanatoriums in various scenic spots where the surroundings are particularly conducive to recuperation from illness.

Throughout the countryside the government has established cooperative medical centers and clinics, which are generally run by production brigades and utilized by peasants on a voluntary basis. They are financed by public welfare funds supplied by the production brigades, money pooled by peasants and the clinics' own operational income.

All persons who seek the services of the cooperative medical centers (including children) need only pay a small sum every year which entitles them to free treatment. If they fall seriously ill and require treatment at a hospital at or below the county level, their medical expenses are paid for either partially or in full by their commune's clinic.

For the past 30 years, special emphasis has been placed on maternity and child care in China. A network of organizations for protecting the health of mothers and children has been established in all cities and throughout the countryside. The Ministry of Public Health has established a Bureau of Maternity and Child Care and a Paediatric Research Institute which operates under the Chinese Academy of Medical Sciences. Besides the gynecological, obstetric and paediatric departments in the general hospitals throughout the provinces. municipalities and autonomous regions, there are maternity hospitals, children's hospitals and maternity and child health centers. The main goal of China's maternity and child health services is the prevention and cure of diseases and complaints common among women and children through the widespread implementation of early medical checkups.

The Chinese government attaches great importance to the prevention and cure of infectious diseases, and in 1952 launched a patriotic health campaign to fight against diseases and unhygienic habits. Infectious diseases which seriously jeopardized the people's health, such as plague, typhoid and typhus, cholera smallpox and venereal diseases, were completely or basically wiped out. The incidence and mortality rate of infectious, parasitic, endemic and occupational diseases has markedly dropped, while the average life span has climbed from a low of 35 years in 1949 to 69 years in 1980.

During the past 30 years, China has made large advances in medical education and research. According to statistics in 1982, there were 112 institutes of higher medical education, 556 secondary medical schools and 282 research institutes of Chinese and Western medicine.

## THE WORLD'S FIRST OPERATION TO REMAKE HANDS BY GRAFTING TOES

In October 1978, a team of surgeons from the Shanghai No. 6 People's Hospital, headed by Yu Zhongjia, the Vice-Director of the Osteology Department, successfully performed the world's first operation to remake hands by grafting toes on a patient who had lost both hands in an accident. Using a man-made metacarpal bone as a support, they dissociated toes from the patient's feet and attached them to this base using micro-surgical techniques. After two years' recuperation, the patient had recovered much of the use of his hands: he had the same sensations of pain, touch and warmth in his new fingers as a normal person; he could make a fist, pinch, twist and drag things with his fingers; carry things not heavier than 35 kilograms; write, button clothing and do other things as well. Since this time doctors in China have successfully performed three other similar operations.

# TRADITIONAL CHINESE MEDICINE

Traditional medicine is an important part of China's cultural heritage; it has a long history and has played an important role in promoting the prosperity of the Chinese race. Before Western medicine entered China on a large scale, beginning in the 1840s, the Chinese people had relied solely on their own traditional medicine.

Traditional Chinese medicine comprises a complete and independent system, the theory and practice of which have been continuously enriched over the course of the past two thousand years.

After the establishment of New China, the Chinese government recognized the importance of developing traditional Chinese medicine and urged that research in the subject should be conducted in a modern scientific way. The ultimate aim of this research was to create a new Chinese medicine by combining elements from both traditional Chinese medicine and Western medical science. From 1949 to 1965 enormous strides were made in

A Traditional Chinese Doctor Feeling a Pulse

A Pharmacy of Traditional Chinese Medicine

this direction. By the end of 1965, there were 280,000 doctors of Chinese medicine working in various medical establishments throughout the country, a group of hospitals of traditional Chinese medicine. A research institute and 21 colleges of traditional Chinese medicine were also set up in that year. Since then these institutions have graduated 5,600 students of traditional Chinese medicine and have provided supplementary training to 4,400 doctors of Western medicine. Research was conducted on some of China's ancient medical texts and these materials were systematized and published, along with a large number of textbooks on traditional medicine and pharmacology.

In 1979, the First Symposium on Traditional Chinese Medicine was held in Beijing. This was not only a historic date in the development of the discipline, but also marked the formal founding of the All-China Society of Traditional Medicine

In addition to advances in acupuncture treatment, there has also been much progress in bone-setting, and now such disorders as slipped disc, disorders of the lower back, joint disorders, and injuries of the soft tissues can be diagnosed and treated satisfactorily, principally through the use of manipulation. A new development in orthopedics is the application of traditional Chinese and Western methods of treatment for fractures and joint injuries. This involves immobilizing the injured limb with small light mobile splints, applying a poultice and prescribing light exercises, at an early stage to hasten healing. This program is carried out in conjunction with the administration of a variety of Chinese medicines, some taken orally and others applied externally. This combined program not only speeds bone healing but also stops pain, reduces swelling and stimulates circulation.

Traditional Chinese medicine has still not found a cure for

cancer, though certain Chinese herbal medicines have proven to be effective in slowing or halting the growth of certain types of cancerous cells.

Traditional Chinese medicine is inseparable from Chinese pharmacology. Each of China's regions has its own distinctive climatic and geological conditions, which give rise to certain native medicinal materials and tonic substances. Among the most well known and widely used are the ginseng and pilose antler of northeast China, the pseudo-ginseng of Yunnan, and the *tianma* (gastrodia clota), bezoar and musk of Sichuan.

China has also achieved some outstanding successes in the field of extracting and process-ing the essence of certain medicinal plants. For example, Chinese scientists have succeed-ed in extracting the essence of the artemisia plant, a substance which is effective in preventing malaria.

In 1977, there were over 400,000 hectares of medicinal plants under cultivation in China, almost twice the amount of similar acreage under cultivation 20 years earlier. More than 56 types of medicinal plants and herbs formerly collected in the wild are now under cultivation in China, *tianma, banxia* (pinellia ternata) and balloon-flower being but three examples.

Chinese medicines have long numbered among China's tradi-tional exports.

## THE WORLD'S FIRST SUCCESSFUL IMPLANTATION OF AN ARTIFICIAL VERTEBRAL SECTION

In June 1970, doctors from the Shanghai Research In-stitute of Traumatology and Osteology and the Ruijin Hospital department of osteology successfully operated on a 27-year-old patient who was suffering from a giant spinal tumor, removing a portion of his spine and replacing it with a stainless steel vertebral section.

Two months after the operation the palsy of the patient's legs disappeared and six months later he was able to stand up. By now, the patient has fully recovered from his former illness and it has been many years since he resumed working.

This operation was performed nine years earlier than the first successful implantation of an artificial vertebra in the United States on July 17, 1979.

# ACUPUNCTURE AND MOXIBUSTION

Among the many inventions and discoveries of Chinese traditional medicine, acupuncture and moxibustion therapy is perhaps the most unique and outstanding. It can be used in the treatment and prevention of a wide variety of illnesses, and has numerous applications in internal medicine, surgery, ophthalmology, otolaryngology, gynecology and paediatrics.

Acupuncture and moxibustion therapy produces rapid results, and is never, or at least very rarely, accompanied by undesirable side-effects.

Acupuncture and moxibustion are two distinct forms of medical treatment, though in both forms, the therapy is carried out on selected acupuncture points based on the therapy of the main and collateral channels (sometimes referred to as meridians). According to this theory, the human body is traversed by a network of main and collateral channels through which the blood and energy (*qi*) circulates. The main channels are called *jing* and the collateral ones are called *luo*. Each of these channels has a definite circulatory route, along which the acupuncture points are distributed. A blockage at any given point along one of these passages is manifested by some particular symptoms. It is on the basis of evidence produced by these symptoms that the doctor makes his diagnosis and then conducts therapeutic treatment.

Acupuncture and moxibustion therapy spread from China to Korea in approximately 600 A.D., and from there spread to Japan and Southeast and Central Asia, finally reaching Europe in the 17th century. At present, extensive research is being done into the scientific basis of acupuncture and moxibustion therapy, while the therapy itself is being practiced in an ever-increasing number of countries throughout the world. However, the acupuncture needles commonly used abroad are the round needles made of gold or silver which were widely in use in China throughout the Ming and Qing dynasties, whereas the needles which have been proven to be the most therapeutically effec-

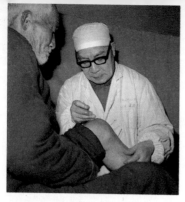

An Acupuncture Treatment

tive are the gold and silver perforated square needles unearthed in Western Han dynasty (206 B.C.-24 A.D.) archaeological sites.

In the past 30 years, great strides have been made in acupuncture therapy. These have led to the discovery of many new acupuncture points and therapeutic methods. As a result, the scope of treatment has now been expanded to include over 300 illnesses, some 100 of which can usually be cured by this method. Among these are acute bacteria dysentrey, certain kinds of paralysis, coronary heart disease and gallstones. Acupuncture is applicable to obstetrics, where it can be used to correct abnormal foetal position and to induce labor.

Acupuncture anaesthesia was invented as the result of centuries of clinical experience in the practice of acupuncture analgesia. The unique feature of operations carried out using this procedure is that the patient remains fully awake during surgery. Because little or no anaesthetics is used, any potential danger arising from its use can be avoided and the patient experiences no unpleasant after-effects. After undergoing an operation in which acupuncture anaesthesia is used, the patient generally experiences only slight post-operational pains and rarely experiences such reactions as nausea and vomiting. Generally speaking, the employment of acupuncture as an anaesthetic technique promotes the quick recovery of the post-operative patient, and in many cases he can resume eating and partaking in most normal activities after a relatively short period of recuperation.

Naturally, acupuncture anaesthesia cannot replace all other forms of anaesthesia, but nevertheless it is an extremely valuable addition to the range of techniques currently available to the anaesthesiologists. Though this form of anaesthesia is now widely used in many kinds of operations, it has proved particularly suitable for those in the region of the neck, head and chest.

# TAIJIQUAN, QIGONG AND OTHER PHYSICAL FITNESS EXERCISES

China's numerous traditional physical fitness exercises may be roughly subdivided into the following basic types: self-massage accomplished by a gentle pummeling of the limbs, exercises to limber up the muscles and joints so as to improve circulation, and others which involve bending or swiveling the waist and moving the other parts of the body so as to stimulate a variety of acupoints.

In China, according to widespread popular legends, one need only take a certain "elixir of immortality" and one will never grow old. In reality, this is sheer fantasy. The only way of ensuring that one will live to a ripe old age is to practice some form of physical exercise on a regular basis.

## TAIJIQUAN

*Taijiquan* originated during the late-Ming or early-Qing period (17th century). As this style of boxing consisted of eight primary hand gestures and five major body movements, it was initially called the "Thirteen Forms". In the late 18th century, the great martial arts master Wang Zongyue wrote a systematic account of this new fighting style, relating it to the classic Chinese philosophy of *yin* and *yang* (the two opposing yet complementary principles in nature), and formally named it *taijiquan*.

Up till one hundred years ago, *taijiquan* was practiced mainly in the countryside of Hunan Province, but by the mid-19th century it had reached Beijing. After being popularized in the capital, it rapidly spread throughout the rest of the country.

Over the past century, *taijiquan* has undergone a variety of changes, with increasing emphasis being placed on the health-building and therapeutic value, and many movements involving explosive thrusts being eliminated. As *taijiquan* evolved, its movements have tended to become more relaxed, smooth and graceful, making it a form of exercise suitable for people of all ages regardless of their physical condition.

There are five major styles of *taijiquan,* among which the Yang school is the most widely practiced and best known. First systematized by Yang Chengfu (1883-1936), its characteristic features are extended and natural postures, slow and even motions, light and steady movements, and flowing lines of performance.

The second most well-known school is the Wu school, first popularized by Wu Jianquan (1870-1942). It is characterized by tightly orchestrated movements executed in a circular pattern.

Third in importance is the Sun school, founded by Sun Lutang (1861-1932). Sun created a style which is characterized by nimble movements performed at a quick tempo and accompanied by lively footwork.

The school with the longest history is the Chen school, first systematized by Chen Faxie (1887-1957). Retaining many elements of the ancient style of Chinese shadow boxing, it is characterized by a combination of vigorous and gentle movements performed in a circular pattern.

Yet another Wu style, also referred to as the Hao style, was established by Wu Xiang (1812-1880). This style is characterized by clearly articulated movements.

In 1956, a simplified set of *taijiquan* exercises based on the most representative sequences of the Yang school was popularized. This series consists of 24 forms which progress from the simplest to the most difficult. The creation of this simplified form of *taijiquan* has done much to bring about a resurgence of interest in the sport, both in China and abroad.

Recently, three other new forms of *taijiquan,* involving cycles of 44, 68 and 88 movements respectively, were created to suit the needs of the more advanced students. More demanding and varied in content, these styles combine traditional *taijiquan* with movements borrowed from traditional Chinese fencing, such as hand pushing and counter-pushing.

## QIGONG

*Qigong* is a form of traditional Chinese breathing exercise which increases vitality and promotes longevity through "regulating the body", "regulating the mind" and "regulating the breath".

The International *Taiji* Champion Ge Chunyan at Practice

*qigong* is an integral part of China's ancient cultural heritage which, because of its importance, has been passed down to the present day.

*Qigong* itself can be subdivided into two forms, a martial form known as "hard *qigong*" and a therapeutic form known as "soft *qigong*". People who have fully mastered the art of breath control (sometimes referred to as "vital energy training") can concentrate their vital energy (*qi*) in various points of their body and render these areas enormously strong and relatively insensitive to pain. Such persons can break stones or iron bars with their feet. *Qigong* masters can support the weight of an automobile with their bodies without being crushed beneath it.

According to textual research carried out by Guo Moruo, former President of the Chinese Academy of Sciences, records of *qigong* can be found in the *jinwen* texts, inscriptions on ancient bronze sacrificial vessels of the Zhou dynasty dating approximately from the 11th century B.C.

China's earliest medical treatise *The Yellow Emperor's Canon of Internal Medicine* makes reference to *qigong* and lists it as one form of therapeutic exercise. The Ming dynasty medical expert Li Shizhen (1518-1593) also mentions *qigong* in his works. Thus

## THERAPEUTIC QIGONG

Recent development in *qigong* is "*waiqi*" or "outflowing energy". This is a form of energy which specially-trained *qigong* masters learn to release through their fingertips. When this energy is directed towards a patient acupoints, it stimulates the body's self-regulating system and can correct a variety of physical imbalances, thereby helping to restore health.

A Group *Taijiquan* Demonstration

## QIGONG PHYSICAL FITNESS EXERCISES

If practiced over a long period of time, *qigong* physical fitness exercises not only can prevent and cure illness, but can also strengthen the physique. *Qigong* has proven to be highly effective in treating certain chronic illnesses which commonly afflict middle-aged and elderly people, such as high blood pressure, coronary heart disease, ulcers, neurasthenia, pains in the lower back and limbs, and chronic upper respiratory infections, and certain soft tissue injuries. There are four main postures used in *qigong* exercises, namely, lying, sitting, standing and walking, but there are essentially only three major techniques: "calming the mind", "concentrating the attention" and "regulating the breath".

The exercise of "calming the mind" can induce inhibitory activity in those areas of the cerebral cortex which control the brain and the rest of the body. This enables the cerebrum to rest and relieves the cerebral cortex of pathological excitation caused by certain ailments, thus helping it to regain its power to regulate the functioning of the body.

If a patient uses the *qigong* technique of "concentrating the attention" to concentrate on his lower abdomen, this can stimulate the nervous system in that area and increase the flow of endocrines in the organs located there.

Frequent practice of the *qigong* technique of "regulating the breath" promotes circulation in the portal veins as well as in the systemic and pulmonary circulatory systems. The net result of this exercise is an increase in the vital capacity of the lungs, improved functioning of the heart and stimulation of metabolism, thus adding in the body's processes of self-repair and self-renewal.

# LIMBERING EXERCISES PERFORMED TO RADIO MUSIC

Limbering exercises performed to radio music are one of the most popular forms of mass athletic activities in China. They subdivide into three sets specially designed for children, young people and adults. Each set consists of exercises for upper limbs, lower limbs and torso, which are performed to the accompaniment of special music broadcast over the radio all over China. These callisthenics are simple and easy to learn, and can be performed almost anywhere. The relatively moderate degree of effort required makes these exercises appropriate for people of all ages.

In 1951, China promulgated its first series of exercises for adults, and this was followed in 1954 by a series of similar exercises for children. After undergoing revisions, the sixth revised set of exercises was

Students at Their Daily Exercise Break

promulgated in 1981. Compared to the earlier exercises, the sixth set is even more effective in limbering up the joints, and goes beyond all previous sets in terms of difficulty.

Since their inception, limbering exercises have become a form of physical exercises which the broad masses of Chinese people look forward to performing every day, especially in schools, offices, factories and mines.

Except on rainy days and Sundays, all Chinese students and pupils in colleges, middle and primary schools participate in these exercises.

In March 1954, the Chinese Government Administrative Council published an announcement concerning the launching of a nationwide physical training movement which stipulated: "In every Chinese work unit, 10 minutes of morning and afternoon work time will be devoted to limbering exercises." Since that time, large numbers of Chinese people have been performing these exercises. Others who prefer traditional Chinese shadow boxing or *taijiquan* may perform a series of such exercises during the 10-minute period.

To facilitate the performance of these exercises, the Central Broadcasting Station and the broadcasting stations of each city and province broadcast the musical accompaniment to the exercises in the morning at 10:00 and in the afternoon at 4:00.

## THE FIRST MATHEMATICAL TREATISE WHICH CITES THE PYTHAGOREAN THEOREM

China's earliest mathematical treatise is titled the *Zhoubisuanjing*. Although its authorship is unknown, archaeologists have placed its publication date sometime during the Western Han dynasty (206 B.C.-24 A.D.). This was one of the earliest mathematical works citing the Pythagorean theorem. Furthermore, it uses a rather complex fractional computational method. Not only is it a pioneering work in the history of Chinese mathematics, but it also occupies a position of importance in the world history of the subject.

# *WUSHU* (MARTIAL ARTS)

*Wushu,* or martial arts, practiced for several thousand years by the people of China for physical training and self-defense, is still highly popular in both the urban and rural areas today. As early as the Zhou dynasty (c. 1066-221 B.C.), *wushu* and archery were included among traditional Chinese sports events. A unique Chinese national sport, *wushu* strengthens the physique, steels the will and teaches fighting skills.

Children at a Martial Arts Training Class

*Wushu* can be divided into four main categories: bare hand Chinese boxing, sword play, boxing duet and group exercise. There are several types of barehand *wushu* exercises, including *changquan* (long boxing), *nanquan* (southern boxing), *taijiquan* (shadow boxing) and *xingyiquan* (imitation boxing). *Changquan* itself is subdivided into many schools, including *Chaquan* (Cha boxing), *Huaquan* (Hua boxing) and *Shaolinquan* (Shaolin boxing). *Taijiquan* subdivides into the Chen, Yang, Wu ( 吴 ), Wu ( 武 ) and Sun schools. *Nanquan* is the collective name of the many schools of boxing widely practiced in southern China, which are based on stylized movements of the dragon, tiger, leopard, snake and crane.

Eight Diagram boxing is based on varied combinations at eight different hand positions or boxing movements derived from the Eight Diagrams (eight combinations of whole or broken lines arranged around a circle formerly used for divination).

*Xingyiquan* (imitation boxing) is based on the movements

of twelve different birds and beasts, including the dragon, tiger, monkey, horse, turtle, chicken, swallow, sparrow, hawk, snake, eagle and panda. *Xiangxingquan* (simulation boxing) imitates both the postures and movements of certain animals, and includes such forms as monkey boxing, preying mantis boxing, eagle talon boxing and snake boxing. There is yet another form which imitates of actions of a drunken person which is sometimes called the "Eight Drunken Immortals" school.

The weapons used in *wushu* exercises are the sword, spear, double-edged sword, club and the nine-sectioned chain and plummet, to name a few. There are also exercises for two people, both armed and unarmed; for one armed fighter and one unarmed fighter; as well as collective exercises, both with and without weapons.

## THE COUNTRY WHICH INVENTED PRINTING BY MOVABLE TYPE

Wood-block printing first appeared in China between the sixth and seventh centuries, approximately 800 years earlier than in Europe. Lithographic printing was also in use in China at this time.

The invention of printing by movable type by Bi Sheng in the period between 1041 and 1048 was a landmark in the history of printing and played a significant role in promoting the dissemination of science and culture in China.

Bi Sheng's major contribution consisted of improving upon the earlier methods of block printing through the use of fired earthenware type, an invention which preceded Gutenberg's printing of the *Latin Bible* with movable type by 400 years.

The principle employed in printing from Bi Sheng's movable type is essentially the same as that employed in modern letterpress technique. In about 1314, Wang Zhen invented movable wooden type and explained its use in his *Methods of Printing from Movable Type,* China's earliest practice on printing technology. Later, bronze type was developed in China as well. During the 14th century the technique of printing with movable type spread throughout China and then disseminated to other parts of the world.

# THE GAME OF GO

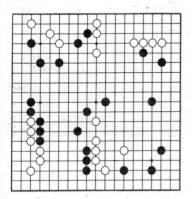

*Go* (in Chinese, *weiqi*) is one form of traditional Chinese chess. Written accounts from as early as the Spring and Autumn and Warring States periods (770-221 B.C.) testify to the game having been played.

*Go* originated in China and spread to Japan during the Tang dynasty (618-907 A.D.). At present, the game is played widely throughout Europe and the Americas.

*Go* is played with 181 black and 180 white pieces (generally flat, round stones) on a square checkered board with 19 vertical lines and 19 horizontal lines forming 361 intersecting points. Each player in turn places his stones on these points. Players compete to conquer territory by surrounding vacant points with their own stones. A single stone, or a group of stones, can be captured and removed from the board if they can be completely encircled by the opponent's stones. Each player's final score is his number of surrounded points less the number of stones lost by capture.

Since 1949, *go* competitions have been held frequently in China. In March 1979, the first World Amateur *Go* Championship was held in Tokyo. The participants came from Europe, America, Oceania, and Asia — a total of 31 contestants from 15 countries and regions. Chinese contestants captured both first and second places in the competition, Nie Weiping winning the championship and Chen Zude coming in second.

*Go* players in China are divided into nine ranks in a system borrowed from Japan. Players above the fifth rank are generally designated as "high-ranking". China has a total of

three players of the ninth rank: Nie Weiping of Sichuan, Chen Zude of Shanghai, and Wu Songsheng, also of Shanghai. China's highest ranking woman *go* player is Kong Xiangming, a sixth-ranking player from Sichuan Province.

## THE CALENDAR SYSTEM IN LONGEST CONTINUOUS USE

China invented a calendar system of the Heavenly Stems and Earthly Branches three to four thousand years ago. It is recorded that the system of the Heavenly Stems and Earthly Branches, designating years from the early Eastern Han dynasty (25-220), has a history of 1,800 years. Compared with the Christian era beginning at Easter day in 532 with 1,400 years' history, the former is 400 or 500 years earlier than the latter.

The system of the Heavenly Stems and Earthly Branches, indicating days from the day of Jisi (the sixth of the Heavenly Stems and Earthly Branches) in February in the third year of the reign of Duke Yin in State of Lu (720 B.C.) to 1911, has a history of more than 2,600 years and provides valuable material for research on calendar making in the ancient world.

# CHINESE CHESS

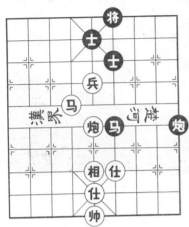

Chinese chess is a traditional Chinese board game which bears many resemblances to Western chess. The game has a long history, its rules having undergone many transformations before they took their present-day form towards the end of the Northern Sung Dynasty (960-1127).

In order to distinguish it from Western chess, this traditional Chinese game has been termed "Chinese chess". Like Western chess, Chinese chess is a game for two players each of whom has sixteen pieces (usually red and black, or red and blue). These pieces include a general, two bodyguards, two elephants, two carriages, two horses, two cannons and five footsoldiers. Each piece has its own designated pattern of movement.

The chessboard is a grid formed by the intersections of nine vertical and ten horizontal lines. The players move their pieces from intersection to intersection, rather than in the squares they form, as in Western chess. The board is further subdivided by a "river" which runs through the center, demarcating each player's territory. The players take turns moving one piece at a time, the object of the game being to capture the opponent's general. In the event that neither player attains this objective, the game is called a draw.

In China, it is estimated that there are roughly 100 million Chinese chess enthusiasts. Many Chinese chess enthusiasts are so

devoted to the game that they play it whenever they can find a stretch of free time. On holidays, Chinese chess competitions and exhibition games are frequently organized. In recent years, Chinese chess has been included among the events in athletic competitions.

Chinese chess is extremely popular in many countries and regions throughout Asia, including the Philippines, Malaysia, Thailand, Japan, Singapore, Hongkong, and Macao. In 1979, the Asian Chinese Chess Association was established, and in each subsequent year it has sponsored an annual Chinese Chess Tournament.

Outstanding players of Chinese chess are divided into the ranks of Grand Master and Master. In China, there are presently two grand masters: Hu Ronghua of Shanghai and Yang Guanlin of Guangdong. Among China's celebrated masters of Chinese chess are Xie Siming, a woman player from Beijing, Li Laiqun of Hebei and Liu Dahua of Hubei.

# TABLE TENNIS IN CHINA

Table tennis in China has developed rapidly since October 1952, when the First National Table Tennis Champi.nships were held in Beijing. According to statistics, about 90 million people throughout China have taken part in this form of sport to date, while the popularity of the sport has led some foreigners to call table tennis China's national sport. Chinese table tennis teams have visited 100 countries and regions in the world, 150 Chinese coaches have been invited by table tennis associations in 74 countries and regions to demonstrate Chinese training and playing techniques.

At the same time many foreign teams have been invited to China. In 1971, the Chinese government's invitation to an American table tennis team marked the restoration of diplomatic relations between the two countries after 20 years, eventually leading to the normalization of relations in 1979. At that time, China's "ping-pong diplomacy" became famous throughout the world.

In 1959, Rong Guotuan be- came the first Chinese to win a world championship. Since then, Chinese players have won 42 world titles (see attached list). In the 36th World Table Tennis Championships held in 1981, the Chinese team won first places in all seven events and second places in five individual events, setting a new record in the 55-year history of the championships.

In 1983, at the 37th World Table Tennis Championships, the Chinese team won the men's team, women's team, men's singles, women's singles, women's doubles and mixed doubles titles.

Children Receiving Training in Table Tennis

## CHINESE WINNERS AT WORLD TABLE TENNIS CHAMPIONSHIPS

| | Men's Team | Women's Team | Singles | | Doubles | | Mixed Doubles |
|---|---|---|---|---|---|---|---|
| | | | Men's | Women's | Men's | Women's | |
| 20th 1953 | Class I-10th place | Class II-3rd place | | | | | |
| 23rd 1956 | Class I-6th place | Class I-11th place | | | | | |
| 24th 1957 | 4th place | 3rd place | | | | | |
| 25th 1959 | 3rd place | 3rd place | Rong Guotuan | | | | |
| 26th 1961 | 1st place | 2nd place | Zhuang Zedong | Qiu Zhonghui | | | |
| 27th 1963 | 1st place | 3rd place | Zhuang Zedong | | Zhang Xielin Wang Zhiliang | | |

| | | | | | | | |
|---|---|---|---|---|---|---|---|
| 28th 1965 | 1st place | 1st place | Zhuang Zedong | | Zhuang Zedong Xu Yinsheng | Lin Huiqing Zheng Minzhi | |
| 31st 1971 | 1st place | 1st place | | Lin Huiqing | | Lin Huiqing Zheng Minzhi | Zhang Xielin Lin Huiqing |
| 32nd 1973 | 2nd place | 2nd place | Xi Enting | Hu Yulan | | | Liang Geliang Li Li |
| 33rd 1975 | 1st place | 1st place | | | | | |
| 34th 1977 | 1st place | 1st place | | | Li Zhenshi Liang Geliang | Yang Ying Bak Iengok (Korean) | |
| 35th 1979 | 2nd place | 1st place | | Ge Xin'ai | | Zhang Deying Zhang Li | Liang Geliang Ge Xin'ai |
| 36th 1981 | 1st place | 1st place | Guo Yuehua | Tong Ling | Li Zhenshi Cai Zhenhua | Zhang Deying Cao Yanhua | Xie Saike Huang Junqun |
| 37th 1983 | 1st place | 1st place | Guo Yuehua | Cao Yanhua | | Dai Lili Shen Jianping | Guo Yuehua Ni Xialian |

The Chinese people's first radio station was the Yan'an Xinhua Broadcasting Station, which commenced operations on January 23, 1940. This station, which went by the call name XNCR, offered only spoken programs and broadcasted on a very limited scale.

After 1949, China's broadcasting industry developed rapidly. By 1979, China had a broadcasting system which included both domestic and overseas radio broadcasts, domestic television broadcasts, and a rural wire-broadcasting network.

China's domestic broadcasting stations include the Central People's Broadcasting Station as well as local broadcasting

## RADIO BROADCASTING STATIONS

stations run by provinces, municipalities, autonomous regions and cities under provincial jurisdiction. Practically all of rural China is wired to one such broadcasting station. In 1982, there were 118 central and local broadcasting stations and 328 relay stations.

The Central People's Broadcasting Station is responsible for promulgating China's Party line and national policies to the entire country, transmitting domestic and overseas features, disseminating cultural and scientific knowledge and offering artistic programs.

China's International Broadcasting Station is responsible for China's overseas broadcasts. Under the name of "Radio Beijing", it broadcasts all over the world for 130 hours a day in 39 foreign languages, and also reaches a large overseas Chinese audience with broadcasts in standard Chinese and four Chinese dialects.

"Radio Beijing" can be picked up on shortwave receivers in almost all regions of the world today.

# A LIST OF CHINA'S MAJOR AM AND FM
## BROADCASTING STATIONS

| Names of Station | AM Band | FM Band |
|---|---|---|
| Central People's Broadcasting Station (I) | 540 567 639 756<br>837 981 1035 1359 | 92.6 94.0 94.2 94.4<br>94.6 94.8 95.6 96.0<br>96.4 96.6 96.8 97.4<br>97.6 97.8 98.0 99.0<br>99.6 99.8 100.0 100.4<br>100.8 101.4 102.2 102.6 |
| Central People's Broadcasting Station (II) | 630 720 855 945<br>1215 1305 | |
| Central People's Broadcasting Station Broadcasts for Taiwan | 594 693 747 909<br>1476 | |
| Beijing People's Broadcasting Station | 828 927 1026<br>1476 | 103.2 |

## SHORTWAVE BROADCASTS OF THE
## CENTRAL PEOPLE'S BROADCASTING STATION

Domestic Radio Broadcasts:

| Programs | GMT | Meter Bands |
|---|---|---|
| First Set of Programs | 20:00 to 17:35<br>the next day | 93 82 67 61 56 51 49 42<br>41 40 39 38 29 25 19 16 |
| Second Set of Programs | 21:00 to 16:00<br>the next day | 91 59 58 50 49 43 41 38<br>31 30 29 25 24 19 16 |
| Programs for Taiwan | 20:00 to 6:00<br>8:30 to 19:00 | 89 62 58 44 32 27 19 |

| Languages | GMT | Regions | Meter Bands |
|---|---|---|---|
| Putonghua (standard Chinese) | 17:30 to 18:30 | West Asia | 49 31 30 25 24 |
| | 20:00 to 21:00 | North Africa, Europe | 42 40 31 26 |
| | 22:30 to 23:00 | Southeast Asia | 51 49 42 30 25 |
| | 02:00 to 03:00 | North America (East Coast) | 25 19 17 16 |
| | 04:00 to 05:00 | North America (West Coast) | 25 19 |
| | 09:00 to 10:00 | Southeast Asia | 32 30 19 16 |
| | 13:00 to 14:00 | Australia, Singapore | 31 25 24 19 16 |
| | 15:00 to 16:00 | South Asia, Southeast Africa | 31 19 |
| Cantonese | 17:00 to 18:00 | South Asia, Southeast Africa | 30 25 19 |
| | 23:00 to 23:30 | Southeast Asia | 51 49 42 30 25 |
| | 1:00 to 2:00 | North America (East Coast) | 25 19 17 16 |
| | 3:00 to 4:00 | North America (West Coast) | 19 16 |
| | 10:00 to 11:00 | Australia, Singapore | 31 24 19 |
| | 11:00 to 12:00 | Southeast Asia | 32 24 19 16 |
| Xiamen (Amoy) Dialect | 23:30 to 24:00 | Southeast Asia, Australia, Singapore | 51 43 32 30 19 24 19 |
| | 12:00 to 13:00 | Australia, Singapore, Southeast Asia | 31 26 16    30 24 19 |
| Kejia (Hakka) Dialect | 17:00 to 18:00 | South Asia, Southeast Africa | 30 25 |
| | 00:00 to 00:30 10:00 to 1:00 | Southeast Asia | 32 24 19 32 19 16 |
| Chaozhou Dialect | 00:30 to 1:00 14:00 to 15:00 | Southeast Asia | 32 30 24 19 16    43 32 31 |

# CHINA'S INTERNATIONAL BROADCASTING

| Languages | GMT | Regions | Meter Bands | | | | |
|-----------|-----|---------|------|------|----|----|----|
| English | 00:00 to 1.00 | North America | 19 | 16 | | | |
| | 1:00 to 2:00 | (East Coast) | 19 | 16 | | | |
| | 2:00 to 3:00 | | 19 | 16 | | | |
| | 3:00 to 4:00 | | 25 | 24 | 19 | 16 | |
| | 12:00 to 13:00 | | 32 | 30 | 25 | 19 | 16 |
| | 3:00 to 4:00 | North America | 25 | 24 | 19 | 16 | |
| | 4:00 to 5:00 | (West Coast) | 25 | 24 | 19 | 16 | |
| | 8:30 to 9:30 | Australia, | 31 | 25 | 19 | 17 | |
| | 9:30 to 10:30 | New Zealand | | | | | |
| | 12:00 to 13:00 | South Asia | 32 | 30 | 25 | 19 | 16 |
| | 13:00 to 14:00 | | | | | | |
| | 14:00 to 15:00 | South Asia | 30 | 25 | 19 | | |
| | 15:00 to 16:00 | | | | | | |
| | 16:00 to 18:00 | East and South Africa, | 30 | 19 | | | |
| | 19:30 to 21:30 | West and North Africa | 39 | 30 | 26 | | |
| | 14:00 to 16:00 | South and Southeast Africa | 30 | 25 | 19 | | |
| | 20:30 to 21:30 | Europe | 49 | 43 | 40 | 26 | |
| | 21:30 to 22:30 | | 49 | 43 | 40 | 26 | |
| | 11:30 to 12:00 | Indo-China | 25 | 19 | | | |
| | 13:00 to 14:00 | | 31 | 25 | | | |

# CHINA'S INTERNATIONAL BROADCASTING

| Languages | GMT | Regions | Meter Bands |
|-----------|-----|---------|-------------|
| French | 18:30 to 19:30 | Africa | 49 45 42 30 25 24 |
| | 20:30 to 21:30 | | |
| | 19:30 to 20:30 | Europe | 49 45 42 30 25 24 |
| | 21:30 to 22:30 | | 49 42 30 25 24 |
| Spanish | 23:00 to 24:00 | Latin America | 49 42 31 30 25 24 19 17 |
| | 00:00 to 01:00 | | 42 31 30 25 24 19 17 16 |
| | 01:00 to 02:00 | | 25 24 19 17 16 |
| | 02:00 to 03:00 | | 49 42 25 24 19 17 16 |
| | 03:00 to 04:00 | | 25 19 |
| | 11:00 to 12:00 | | 30 25 19 |
| | 20:30 to 21:30 | Europe | 40 31 25 |
| Japanese | 21:30 to 22:00 | Japan | 43 40 26 |
| | 0:30 to 15:00 | | |
| Arabic | 16:30 to 17:30 | North Africa, | 43 40 31 26 |
| | 18:30 to 19:30 | West Asia | |
| German | 18:00 to 19:00 | Central Europe | 49 42 38 26 |
| | 20:00 to 21:00 | | |
| Russian | 10:00 to 22:00 | Europe and Asia | 49 41 31 25 19 16 |
| | 21:00 to 22:30 | | |
| | 23:00 to 5:00 | | |

# TELEVISION STATIONS

The main purpose of the television stations of the People's Republic of China is to transmit news broadcasts, to promulgate government directives, to spread cultural and scientific knowledge as well as to provide entertainment.

The China Central Television Station (CCTV), formerly known as the Beijing Television Station, was the first station founded in China. In May 1958, CCTV launched a series of trial broadcasts, and in September of the same year began broadcasting officially. CCTV adopted its present name in May 1978. Prior to 1973, it only broadcast on one channel, and all transmissions were in black and white. At that time, except for a small number of news and educational programs, it broadcast mainly films, theatrical performances and sports events.

CCTV made its first trial color broadcasts in May 1973. Four years later, it commenced color broadcasts on two channels. The first channel broadcast to Beijing and was also transmitted by microwave relay to television stations throughout China. The second channel broadcast locally in the city of Beijing and its environs.

In 1979, CCTV, in conjunction with the Ministry of Education, established the Central Television University. At present, CCTV broadcasts three sets of television programs on two channels.

CCTV is administered directly by the Ministry of Radio and Television Broadcasting. At present, CCTV has a staff of nearly 1,000, 35 percent of whom work as editors, broadcasters, Photographers, television cameramen, composers and artists, 40 percent as technicians, 15 percent as general workers, and the remaining ten percent as administrative personnel.

At present, every province and autonomous region in China, as well as Beijing, Shanghai and Tianjin (the three municipalities directly under the Central Government) has its own television station which broadcasts local programs, in addition to relaying CCTV programs.

# CHINA'S MAJOR TELEVISION CHANNELS

| Stations | Location | Channels |
|----------|----------|----------|
| Central Television Station | Beijing | 2, 8 |
| | Shanghai | 8 |
| | Tianjin | 5 |
| | Changchun | 7 |
| | Harbin | 8 |
| | Wuhan | 8 |
| | Guangzhou | 8 |
| | | |
| Regional Stations | | |
| | | |
| Beijing | Beijing | 6 |
| Tianjin | Tianjin | 12 |
| Hebei | Shijiazhuang | 1 |
| Shanxi | Taiyuan | 5 |
| Inner Mongolia | Hohhot | 2 |
| Liaoning | Shenyang | 5 |
| Jilin | Changchun | 2 |
| Heilongjiang | Harbin | 1 |
| Shandong | Jinan | 2 |
| Shanghai | Shanghai | 5, 20 |
| Jiangsu | Nanjing | 1 |
| Anhui | Hefei | 5 |
| Zhejiang | Hangzhou | 4 |
| Jiangxi | Nanchang | 5 |
| Fujian | Fuzhou | 2 |
| Henan | Zhengzhou | 2 |
| Hubei | Wuhan | 4 |
| Hunan | Changsha | 1 |
| Guangdong | Guangzhou | 2, 14 |
| Guangxi | Nanning | 4 |
| Shaanxi | Xi'an | 8 |
| Ningxia | Yinchuan | 4 |
| Gansu | Lanzhou | 4 |
| Qinghai | Xining | 4 |
| Xinjiang | Urumqi | 5 |
| Sichuan | Chengdu | 2 |
| Guizhou | Guiyang | 4 |
| Yunnan | Kunming | 2 |
| Tibet | Lhasa | 4 |

# FILMS AND FILM AWARDS

The Chinese film industry was first established in 1913, but up until 1949 film making was entirely confined to a few large cities and developed very slowly. The founding of the People's Republic of China gave a great impetus to the industry's development.

Within a short period of time, great strides were made both in the number and quality of the films and they began to draw international recognition. By 1962, 63 Chinese films had received awards at various international film festivals, including 20 feature films, 16 puppet films and cartoons, 17 documentary films and 10 scientific educational films.

The One Hundred Flowers Film Award was established in 1962 in order to commend achievement in film production, form closer links between the audience and the film industry and subject the films directly to the appraisal of the masses. The award comprises over a dozen of prizes, including prizes for best actor, actress, supporting actor or actress and director; prizes for best feature films, documentary films and musicals; as well as prizes for best film script, shooting and so forth. The winners of these prizes are decided by popular vote, the ballots being distributed by *Dazhong Dianying*, the most popular national film magazine in China.

However, the award was held only twice before it was discontinued for 17 years, owing to the vicious interference of the Gang of Four during the "cultural revolution". The downfall of the Gang in 1976 paved the way for a second surge of development in China's film industry. Virtually deprived of any film entertainment during the whole course of the "cultural revolution", the masses showed unprecedented interest in the development of the film industry and demanded the restoration of the One Hundred Flowers Award. In 1980, the Third One Hundred Flowers Award was held, with a record of 1.5 million people participating in the voting. When the

The Third One Hundred Flowers Award Ceremony

fourth one was held the next year, over 2 million people took part.

At the same time, the total number of China's film studios grew to over 20 and great headway was made in the annual turnout of films. 1980 saw the production of 82 feature films, 32 puppet films and cartoons, 365 documentary films and 337 scientific educational films.

With the ever increasing output of the Chinese film industry and growing interest of the nation's audiences, the question of improving the quality of the films has come to the fore. It was with a view to raising the overall quality of Chinese films as well as the professional and ideological level of people engaged in film production that in 1981 the Chinese Film Artists' Association decided to establish a Golden Rooster Film Award. The Golden Rooster Award comprises 20 prizes, including prizes for best feature, documentary, scientific educational, puppet films and cartoons and musicals; prizes for best actor, actress, supporting actor and actress and best director; as well as prizes for best movie scripts, shooting and so forth. However, unlike the One Hundred Flowers Award, the awarding of these prizes is decided by an Award Assessment Committee, a panel composed of China's most prominent film critics and specialists.

The One Hundred Flowers Award has proven to be an effective means of letting the audience identify themselves with film production, while the Golden Rooster Award has done much to raise the technical and ideological awareness of persons engaged in film production, allowing them to have their work appraised by experts. Collectively, the two film awards are playing an important role in promoting the development of the Chinese film industry, encouraging the production of films which not only serve China's socialist construction but which also meet the highest international standards of film making.

## THE WORLD'S FIRST SPANDREL ARCH BRIDGE

The Anji Bridge, also known as the Zhaozhou Bridge, spans the Xiaohe River in Zhaoxian County, Hebei Province. It was built by Li Chun sometime between the years 590 and 608 A.D. The bridge consists of one arch; it is 59 meters long, 9.6 meters wide at both ends and 9 meters wide in the middle. The span of its arch is 37.37 meters; the rise from the chord-line to the crown is a mere 7 meters and the ratio of the span of the arch to its crown is not more than 5:1, giving the bridge's surface an unprecedentedly gentle curve, in contradistinction to the semi-circular form which had been previously in use. The bridge's floor was laid using rectangular stone slabs 30 cm. thick and its arch was constructed from 28 stone slabs. The brilliance of the bridge's engineering work can most clearly be seen in the two semi-circular openings in either to the bridge's arch spandrels which simultaneously reduce the weight of the upper portion of the bridge, economize on construction materials, facilitate flood drainage and enhance the bridge's aesthetic effect.

The Anji Bridge represents a number of remarkable advances in bridge construction engineering: not only does it have the gentlest curve and longest span of any bridge in the ancient world but it is also the world's first spandrel arch bridge.

## PRIZES AWARDED TO CHINESE FEATURE FILMS AT INTERNATIONAL FILM FESTIVALS SINCE 1949

| Recipient of Award | Date of Award | Place | Name of Film Festival and Type of Award |
|---|---|---|---|
| "Daughters of China" | July, 1950 | Czechoslovakia | The Fifth International Karlovy Vary Film Festival, won the fourth of five "People's Liberation Struggle Prizes" |
| Actress: Shi Lianxing "Chao Yiman" | July, 1950 | Czechoslovakia | The Fifth International Karlovy Vary Film Festival, Best Acting Award |
| "Steeled Fighter" | July, 1951 | Czechoslovakia | The Sixth International Karlovy Vary Film Festival, won the second of five "Peace Prizes" |
| "White-Haired Girl" | July, 1951 | Czechoslovakia | The Sixth International Karlovy Vary Film Festival, Special Award |
| Director: Shi Dongshan "The New Heroic Sons and Daughters" | July, 1951 | Czechoslovakia | The Sixth International Karlovy Vary Film Festival, Special Award for Direction |
| Cinematographer: Feng Zizhi "Red Banner over Mount Cuikang" | July, 1952 | Czechoslovakia | The Seventh International Karlovy Vary Film Festival, Photography Award |

| | | | |
|---|---|---|---|
| Screenwriter:<br>Wang Chenzhi<br>"The Victory of the People<br>of Inner Mongolia" | July, 1952 | Czechoslovakia | The Seventh International Karlovy Vary Film Festival, Screenplay Award |
| "The People's Soldier" | July, 1952 | Czechoslovakia | The Seventh International Karlovy Vary Film Festival, the "Struggle for Freedom Award" |
| "Taking Huashan Mountain by Strategy" | July, 1954 | Czechoslovakia | The Eighth International Karlovy Vary Film Festival, the "Struggle for Freedom Award", one of the seven principal awards |
| "Liang Shanbo and Zhu Yingtai" | July, 1954 | Czechoslovakia | The Eighth International Karlovy Vary Film Festival, Musical Film Award |
| "Liang Shanbo and Zhu Yingtai" | 1955 | Ireland | The Ninth International Edinburgh Film Festival, won Outstanding Film Award |
| "The Letter with Feathers" | 1955 | Ireland | The Ninth International Edinburgh Film Festival, won Outstanding Film Award |
| "Woman Basketball Player No. 5" | June, 1957 | Soviet Union | The Sixth International Youth Film Festival, Silver Award |
| "New Year's Sacrifice" | July, 1957 | Czechoslovakia | The Tenth International Karlovy Vary Film Festival, Special Award |
| Actor: Da Qi<br>Actress: Wang Xiaotang<br>"Skirmishes on the Border" | July, 1958 | Czechoslovakia | The Eleventh International Karlovy Vary Film Festival, Young Actors Award |

183

PRIZES AWARDED TO CHINESE FEATURE FILMS AT INTERNATIONAL
FILM FESTIVALS SINCE 1949 (CONTINUED)

| Recipient of Award | Date of Award | Place | Name of Film Festival and Type of Award |
| --- | --- | --- | --- |
| "The Soul of the Sea" | July, 1959 | Czechoslovakia | The Tenth Working People's Film Festival, "The Second Class Struggle for World Peace Award" |
| "The New Story of an Old Soldier" | August, 1959 | Soviet Union | The First Moscow International Film Festival, Silver Award for Technical Achievements |
| Actress: Yang Likun Director: Wang Jiaji "Five Golden Flowers" | March, 1960 | Egypt | The Second Cairo African-Asian Film Festival, Silver Eagle Award for best actress, Silver Eagle Award for best director |
| "Nie Er" | July, 1960 | Czechoslovakia | The Twelfth International Karlovy Vary Film Festival, Biographical Film Award |
| Actress: Yu Lan "A Revolutionary Family" | July, 1961 | Soviet Union | The Second Moscow International Film Festival, Best Actress Award |
| "The Manlo Flower" | July, 1963 | Switzerland | The Sixteenth International Locarno Film Festival, Certificate of Merit |
| Actor: Chen Qiang "The Red Detachment of Women" | April, 1964 | Indonesia | The Third Asian-African Film Festival, Best Actor Award |

| | | | |
|---|---|---|---|
| "The Battle of the Mines" | April, 1974 | Austria | Vienna Commemorative Award |
| Actress: Yuan Xia "The Unfailing Beam" | July, 1978 | Yugoslavia | The Yugoslavia International Film Festival, Best Actress Award |
| "Two Actresses" | 1981 | Philippines | Manila Film Festival, "Golden Eagle Award" |
| "Serfs" | 1981 | Philippines | Manila Film Festival, "Golden Eagle Award" |
| "The Young Teacher" | 1981 | India | The Second Indian International Children's Film Festival, Best Children's Film Award |
| "The Plum Flower Embroidery" | January, 1981 | Philippines | The First International Manila Film Festival, "Special Award" |
| "The Legend of Tianyun Mountain" | March, 1982 | Hongkong | The First Hongkong Jin Xiang Film Festival, Best Film Award |
| "Anxious to Return" | March, 1982 | Hongkong | The First Hongkong Jin Xiang Film Festival, Best Film Award |
| "Ashima" | July, 1982 | Spain | The Third Santander Dance Movie Festival, Dance Film Award |
| "Four Buddies" | July, 1982 | Italy | The Thirteenth International Giffoni Young People's Film Festival, received the highest honor of the President of the Republic Silver Award |
| Actor: Yan Shunkai "The True Story of Ah Q" | August, 1982 | Switzerland | The Second International Vevey Comedy Film Festival, Best Actor Award |

## GOLDEN ROOSTER AWARDS

|  | 1981 | 1982 | 1983 |
|---|---|---|---|
| Best Feature Films | "Evening Rain", "The Legend of Tianyun Mountain" | "Neighbors" | "At Middle Age", "Rickshaw Boy" |
| Best Screen Writer Award | Ye Nan for the screenplay of "Evening Rain" | Zhang Xuan for the screenplay of "A Corner Forgotten by Love" | |
| Best Director Award | Xie Jin for his direction of "The Legend of Tianyun Mountain" | Cheng Yin for his direction of "The Xi'an Incident" | Wu Yigong for his direction of "My Memories of Old Beijing" |
| Best Actor Award | | Zhang Yan for his portrayal of Jiang Maofu in "Laughter in Moon Village" | |
| Best Actress Award | Zhang Yu for her portrayal of Zhou Yun in "Romance on Mount Lushan" | Li Xiuming for her portrayal of Xu Xiuyun in "Xu Mao and His Daughters" | |

| Best Supporting Actors or Actresses | Shi Ling<br>for his portrayal of the old artisan in "Evening Rain" | Sun Feihu<br>for his portrayal of Chiang Kai-shek in "The Xi'an Incident" | Zheng Zhenyao<br>for her portrayal of Song Ma in "My Memories of Old Beijing" |
| --- | --- | --- | --- |
| | Quyang Ruji<br>for her portrayal of the old mother — same film | He Xiaoshu<br>for his portrayal of Ling Hua in "A Corner Forgotten by Love" | Niu Ben<br>for his portrayal of Guo Piazi in "The Herdsman" |
| | Lin Bin<br>for his portrayal of the teacher — same film | | |
| | Zhong Xinghuo<br>for his portrayal of the policeman — same film | | |
| | Mao Weihui<br>for her portrayal of the little girl — same film | | |
| | Lu Qing<br>for his portrayal of the young worker — same film | | |

LIST OF RECIPIENTS OF CHINA'S ONE HUNDRED FLOWERS AWARD

| | 1962 | 1963 | 1980 | 1981 | 1982 | 1983 |
|---|---|---|---|---|---|---|
| Best Feature Film | "The Red Detachment of Women" | "Li Shuangshuang" | "Ji Hongchang", "Tear Stains", "Small Flower" | "Romance on Mount Lushan", "The Legend of Tianyun Mountain", "A Minor Official" | "In-Law", "Call of the Home Village", "The White Snake" | "At Middle Age", "The Herdsman", "The Rickshaw Boy" |
| Best Actor | Cui Wei portraying Zhu Laozhong in "The Song of the Red Flag" | Zhang Liang portraying Dahu and Erhu in "Two Brothers" | Li Rentang portraying Zhu Keshi in "Tear Stains" | Da Shichang portraying Lin Hanhua in "The Swallows' Return" | Wang Xingang portraying Cai E in "Intimate Friends" | Yen Shunkai portraying Ah Q in "The True Story of Ah Q" |
| Best Actress | Zhu Xijuan portraying Wu Qinghua in "The Red Detachment of Women" | Zhang Ruifang portraying Li Shuangshuang in "Li Shuangshuang" | Chen Chong portraying Xiaohua in "Little Flower" | Zhang Yu portraying Zhou Yun in "Romance on Mount Lushan" | Li Xiuming portraying Xu Xiuyun in "Xu Mao and His Daughters" | Siqingaowa portraying Hu Niu in "The Rickshaw Boy" |
| Award for Best Supporting Actor or Actress | Chen Qiang portraying Nan Batian in "The Red Detachment of Women" | Zhong Xinghuo portraying Sun Xiwang in "Li Shuangshuang" | Liu Xiaoqing portraying Zhang Lan in "Look at This Family" | | | Niu Ben portraying Guo Piazi in "The Herdsmen" Jiang Lili portraying Ye Fang in "The Colors of the Rainbow" |

# THE WORLD'S LARGEST PALACE

The Palace Museum, originally known as the Forbidden City, is a group of palaces in the heart of Beijing constructed along the city's north-south axis. The construction of the palace complex was begun in the fourth year of the Yongle reign (1406) of the Ming dynasty and was completed 14 years later. Twenty-four emperors lived there over a span of 491 years, during the course of which time the building complex was repeatedly expanded and refurbished.

The grand palace buildings were not only splendid in appearance but were well protected by multiple lines of defense. The battlemental wall which surrounds the palace complex is ten meters high and extends 760 meters from east to west and 960 meters from north to south, enclosing an area of 720,000 square meters. At each corner of the wall is a three-storied watch tower and outside is a moat 52 meters wide. Within the palace complex there are 9,999 buildings (a number symbolizing long life and long reign for the emperor) laid out around several dozen courtyards. The main palace buildings are on the meridian line facing south, and the less important buildings range from east to west. Wumen, the main and south gate to the palace, is the complex's most impressive portal, with three great walls more than ten meters high and five massive towers.

With its magnificent halls and courtyards and its imperial collection of artwork and antiques, the whole palace is one of the major world museums of Chinese history, culture and art. Furthermore, it is the world's largest and most complete palace complex which has survived entirely intact down to the present day.

# NATIONAL NEWSPAPERS PUBLISHED IN BEIJING

*Renmin Ribao (People's Daily)*

*Renmin Ribao* is the organ of the Central Committee of the Chinese Communist Party. During the period encompassed by the Second Revolutionary Civil War,* the War of Resistance Against Japan and the Third Revolutionary Civil War** the Central Committee of the CCP successively published three newspapers: *Red Flag, New China Daily* and *Liberation Daily.* In 1947, *Liberation Daily* ceased publication and was replaced by *Renmin Ribao,* which became the official organ of the North China Bureau of the Party Central Committee.

*Renmin Ribao* began publication at Xibaipo, Pingshan County, Hebei Province, in what was then North China Liberated Area. It moved from there to Shijiazhuang, the capital of Hebei, and then to Beijing where it commenced publication in January 1949. It became the official organ of the Party Central Committee in August of the same year.

*Renmin Ribao* reports to readers at home and abroad on Party and government policies and positions. It covers domestic and international news events, discusses theoretical issues, and reports on progress in Party building work and the activities of the mass organizations for workers, youth and women. It popularizes achievements in the fields of

---

* The Second Revolutionary Civil War is also known as the "Ten-Year Civil War" or the "Agrarian Revolution War". It refers to the ten-year struggle waged by the Chinese people under the leadership of the Chinese Communist Party against the reactionary Chiang Kai-shek clique during the years from 1927 to 1937. The hostilities commenced on April 12, 1927, in Shanghai when Chiang Kai-shek launched a counter-revolutionary coup, destroying the alliance between the Kuomintang and the Communist Party.

** The Third Revolutionary Civil War is also known as the "War of Liberation". It refers to the four-year struggle waged by the Chinese people under the leadership of the Communist Party from 1945 to 1949 to overthrow the reactionary Kuomintang regime, ending ultimately in the founding of the People's Republic of China.

economics, culture, science and education. The paper also publishes letters from readers.

All articles in *Renmin Ribao* follow the line of the Central Committee of the Chinese Communist Party and reflect the fundamental interests of the masses.

*Renmin Ribao* appears daily in an eight-page folio edition. The first and fourth pages carry major domestic news items, commentaries and news dispatches. The second page carries economic news, the third page political, cultural and educational news items, the fifth page theoretical and political articles, articles on literature and art as well as letters from readers, the sixth and seventh pages carry international news, and the eighth carries special supplements.

*Renmin Ribao* has seven daily columns: "Daily Discussion", "Letters from Readers", "Market Notes", "Newspaper and Magazine Digest", "News Analysis", "International Notes" and the "World of Sports".

The paper has a daily circulation of approximately five million copies. Besides being published in Beijing, it is also published in 21 other Chinese cities as well as Hongkong and Tokyo by means of satellite transmission or by air delivery of full-page plate-molds. The publication of an American edition in San Francisco began in 1982. The paper is distributed in 122 countries and regions in the world.

The *Renmin Ribao* Publishing House also publishes three other newspapers: *The Market, Humor and Satire* and *Newsfront.*

*The Market (Shichang)* is a weekly economic journal with a nationwide scope. It is intended for both producers and consumers and carries reports on the state of the national economy as well as marketing news from home and foreign sources. It is printed in color in an eight-page quarto edition and has a circulation of about 500,000.

*Humor and Satire (Fengci yu Youmo)*, the cartoon supplement of *Renmin Ribao*, commenced publication in January 1979. It is printed in color in a semi-monthly four-page quarto edition. Its present circulation is one million.

*Newsfront (Xinwen Zhanxian)* is a comprehensive journal devoted to journalism and the journalistic profession in China. It publishes both theoretical and educational articles on the subject.

### China Daily

*China Daily*, the first and only national daily English language newspaper which has been established in China since the founding of the People's Republic, first commenced publication on June 1, 1981.

Besides a Beijing edition, it also has a Hongkong edition and a North American edition. At its start, the paper had a daily circulation of 10,000 copies, but by December 1983 this figure had grown to over 70,000. It is published in eight standard-sized pages and is distributed to 120 countries.

The front page features news of the major developments of the day; page 2 carries economic and financial news, both domestic and foreign. Page 3 carries domestic news and page 4 is the opinion page, carrying translations of commentaries and articles from *Renmin Ribao* and other leading Chinese publications, as well as editorials written by *China Daily's* own commentators. Page 5 is the culture page, and is devoted to feature articles on Chinese art, drama, music, science, medicine and tourism. Page 6 is the life/people page, and it provides portraits of people from various walks of life as well as featuring contract bridge and crossword puzzle columns and listings of radio and television programs, exhibitions, film shows, and theatrical and concert performances. Page 7 is devoted to sports news, both international and domestic; the eighth and last page is devoted entirely to world news.

## Jiefangjun Bao (People's Liberation Army Daily)

Jiefangjun Bao is the organ of the Central Military Affairs Committee of the Chinese Communist Party. It is run directly by the Committee's General Political Department and has a total daily circulation of 1.5 million.

## Guangming Ribao (Enlightenment Daily)

Guangming Ribao began publication in Beijing on June 16, 1949, as the organ of the Central Committee of the All-China Democratic League. At the end of 1952 it became the combined organ of all the democratic parties. Its articles

are primarily concerned with science, education, Marxist theory, literature and art, with a readership composed of a broad range of intellectuals. The paper is distributed both at home and abroad. In 1981, its average daily circulation was approximately 1.06 million.

## Gongren Ribao (Workers' Daily)

Gongren Ribao is the organ of the All-China Federation of Trade Unions. It began publication on July 15, 1949, in Beijing, and in 1979 the State Economic Commission commenced participating in its leadership. Gongren Ribao is a comprehensive daily newspaper with a readership consisting of the broad masses of Chinese workers in industry, transportation, construction, agriculture, forestry, culture and education, and finance and trade. It is also read widely by engineers and technicians in these fields as well as all ranks of cadres and management personnel. In 1981, its average circulation was 1.82 million.

## Zhongguo Qingnian Bao (Chinese Youth)

Zhongguo Qingnian Bao is the organ of the Chinese Communist Youth League. The paper was founded on April 27, 1951, in Beijing. At first, it was a folio newspaper published twice a week. However, in 1981 it commenced issuing four editions per week and an 8-page Sunday supplement. *Zhongguo Qingnian Bao* caters to the interests of China's young people and offers solutions to the problems they encounter in life. At present, it has a circulation of 2.9 million, a portion of which is sent to overseas subscribers.

### Zhongguo Nongmin Bao (Chinese Peasant Gazette)

*Zhongguo Nongmin Bao* is a comprehensive newspaper written in simple language for peasants. It began publication on April 6, 1980, in Beijing and is now published in a bi-weekly quarto edition with eight pages per issue. The paper is edited under the direct leadership of the State Agricultural Commission. Its readers are the broad masses of Chinese commune members, including rural cadres and management personnel. Besides carrying articles concerning Chinese current events, *Zhongguo Nongmin Bao* also covers a wide range of subjects of interest to Chinese rural dwellers, such as new developments in agriculture, forestry, husbandry and fishery.

### Zhongguo Fazhi Bao (Chinese Legal Gazette)

*Zhongguo Fazhi Bao* was founded on August 1, 1980. It is the nation's only publicly distributed journal concerning politics and law. The major task of this journal is to report on policies and other measures being implemented by China to strengthen its legal system, to propagate the Constitution and the government's legal directives, to disseminate knowledge concerning the nation's laws, and to report on achievements in building the socialist legal system. At present, the journal is published once a week. When the journal was first established on August 1, 1980, its circulation was 1.1 million. However, by December 1981, its circulation had risen to 5.3 million. *Zhongguo Fazhi Bao* has subscribers in several dozen countries in the world as well as in Hongkong and Macao.

### Zhongguo Caimao Bao (Chinese Finance and Trade)

*Zhongguo Caimao Bao* was founded on July 4, 1978, in Beijing under the original name *Tradefront*. At the time of its founding it was published twice weekly in a quarto edition. In 1979, however, it became a folio. On January 1, 1981, it adopted its present name, commenced publication on a thrice-weekly basis, and also began to be distributed abroad.

*Zhongguo Caimao Bao* is an economic journal of national scope edited by the Finance and Trade Group of the State Council. The journal is read widely by the nation's 15 million financial and economic workers. It publishes reports concerning Chinese commerce, foreign trade, marketing and supply, industrial management, public finance, taxation, financial administration, commodity price supervision, aquatic products, and the supply of grain and food staples. At the same time, it also carries articles promoting China's light industry and its textile and tourist industries.

The present weekly circulation of *Zhongguo Caimao Bao* is one million copies, with several hundred copies being distributed abroad. Besides that published in Beijing, editions are published in Shanghai, Wuhan, Xi'an, Chengdu, Guangzhou and Kunming.

## Tiyu Bao (Sports)

*Tiyu Bao* commenced publication on a trial basis in July 1956. After 12 issues, it began formal publication in September 1959. It is published by the State Physical Culture and Sports Commission. At present, it is published four times a week in a four-page folio edition.

*Tiyu Bao* is China's only nationwide athletic newspaper. It caters to the needs and interests of the masses and is aimed at promoting the national spirit and encouraging interest in sports and other athletic activities. It carries timely reports on major athletic contests at home and abroad. It frequently reports on group athletic activities and furnishes information concerning exercises which promote health and physical fitness. The circulation of *Tiyu Bao* has increased since its founding. In 1981, its circulation ranged from 447,000 to 556,000 copies per issue. The average circulation for the year was 497,380.

Besides the above-mentioned newspapers, other national newspapers published in Beijing include *Jiankang (Health), Renmin Tiedao Bao (People's Railroads), Renmin Youdian (People's Post and Telecommunications), Tuanjie Bao (Unity)* and *Zhongguo Shaonian Bao (Chinese Children),* the last-named having the largest circulation of any newspaper in the country.

# CHINA'S FOREIGN LANGUAGES PUBLISHING ESTABLISHMENTS AND FOREIGN LANGUAGES PERIODICALS

## FOREIGN LANGUAGES PRESS

Established in November 1949, under the title of the Information Bureau of the Press Administration, the Foreign Languages Press (FLP) took its present name after the bureau's reorganization in 1952. From its inception up till 1963, the Foreign Languages Press had as its task the publication and distribution of Chinese books and periodicals in foreign translation. In 1963, the FLP was incorporated into the newly founded Foreign Languages Publication and Distribution Bureau, and since then has been responsible solely for the translation and publication of books only.

Over the past 30 years the Press has published works of Marx, Engels, Lenin and Stalin; works of Mao Zedong; documents of the Chinese Communist Party and the People's Republic of China; theoretical and political works; works providing general information about China; literary works and postcards and pictorial albums. The FLP publishes in 14 foreign languages: English, French, Spanish, Russian, German, Japanese, Arabic, Korean, Thai, Hindi, Urdu, Portuguese, Swahili, and Bengali.

While continuing to publish the above-mentioned books, the FLP will place greater emphasis on publishing books which provide general information about China, including works on history, geography, economy, art and culture, health and education, as well as books and pictorial albums concerning the Chinese people's modernization drive.

All books published by the FLP are distributed by China International Book Trading Corporation (Guoji Shudian) to 171 countries and regions.

## NEW WORLD PRESS

At its inception, the New World Press only published books written by foreign authors concerning China's

politics, diplomatic affairs, economy, social conditions, culture, art, literature and history, and distributes them both domestically and abroad. Since it was established in 1951, it has published works in English by Anna Louise Strong, Israel Epstein, Rewi Alley, Jack Chen and a number of other foreign writers. Some of these books have also appeared in French, German, Spanish and Arabic editions.

Since 1979, the New World Press has expanded the scope of its activities to include the publication of foreign language books by Chinese authors as well as Chinese books in English translation, primarily nonfictional works dealing with various facets of Chinese culture and life in contemporary China.

All the publications of the New World Press are distributed abroad by the China International Book Trading Corporation (C.I.B.T.C.).

## FOREIGN LANGUAGES PRINTING HOUSE

Established in January 1951, the Foreign Languages Printing House accepts orders from both home and abroad to print books and periodicals in foreign languages. The printing house handles more than 50 languages. Except for Chinese, Japanese, Korean, Kampuchean and Lao, which are hand-set, mechanical composition is available for all the other languages. Computerized photocomposition is also available for English, French, Spanish, German, Romanian, Italian, Portuguese and Swedish.

The Foreign Languages Printing House has eight workshops which respectively handle composition, stereotype, rotary offset, offset, photogravure, binding, plates and machine-repair.

## CHINA INTERNATIONAL BOOK TRADING CORPORATION (GUOJI SHUDIAN)

China International Book Trading Corporation (C.I.B.T.C.) is a foreign trade organization which specializes in books and periodicals. It was first established in December 1949, as an import-export firm, but from 1964 to 1981 it specialized in the export of Chinese publications. Today, to meet the home market's growing need for foreign literature, it has once again taken up the import of foreign publications.

Books, periodicals, newspapers, microprints head the list of exports of C.I.B.T.C., augmented over the years by an increasing variety of art items such as original paintings, woodblock prints, folk papercuts, phonograph records and cassette tapes.

The export of Chinese publications has kept pace with China's fast-developing economic and cultural relations with other countries. During the past three decades, C.I.B.T.C. has supplied overseas markets with thousands of titles and millions of copies of publications of all descriptions, including Marxist-Leninist works, Mao Zedong's writings, classical and modern works of art and literature, documentary works, picture albums and books providing background information about China.

In addition, it distributes a large number of periodicals in foreign languages, hundreds of Chinese language newspapers and periodicals.

All publications of the New World Press are distributed by C.I.B.T.C., which has over 800 sales agents abroad, maintains direct relations with hundreds of thousands of individual readers and subscribers, and exports to 171 countries and regions all over the world.

### CHINA PICTORIAL

*China Pictorial* is a comprehensive, large-format monthly

magazine. The Chinese edition commenced publication in July 1950, the English edition in January 1951, and the Russian edition in July 1951. After *China Pictorial* was incorporated into the Foreign Languages Press in 1953, many new foreign language editions were added. In 1959, it was changed into a fortnightly, but in 1961 resumed publication as a monthly.

The magazine is now published in 19 languages: Chinese, Mongolian, Tibetan, Uygur, Kazak, Korean, Russian, English, German, French, Japanese, Hindi, Spanish, Arabic, Swahili, Swedish, Italian, Urdu and Romanian.

The magazine's pictorial reports cover China's socialist construction and the life of its various nationalities. The magazine also regularly reports on China's political, economic and cultural affairs and the achievements of its people in their modernization drive. It also carries several regular columns such as "Works of Art" and "Tourist Guide".

Size: 8-mo
48 pages, about half in color
Distributed by C.I.B.T.C. to 130 countries and regions

## CHINA RECONSTRUCTS

Founded by Soong Ching Ling (Mme. Sun Yat-sen, 1893-1981) and published by the China Welfare Institute, *China Reconstructs* is an illustrated monthly covering a wide range of general subjects. When it commenced publication in 1952, the magazine initially appeared only in English. However, after 1960, Spanish, French, Arabic, Russian and German editions were successively added (the Russian edition ceased publication in 1978). For the benefit of overseas Chinese readers, a Chinese edition was added in October 1980. And a North American edition has been published beginning January 1983.

*China Reconstructs* is dedicated to the reporting about the building of socialism in China, the life of its people and their accomplishments. The goal of the magazine is to promote understanding and friendship between the Chinese people and the people of other countries. Besides reflecting how the Chinese people are striving to build their land into a powerful, modern socialist country, its articles also provide background information concerning Chinese history, geography and culture.

The magazine carries such regular columns as "In Our Society", "Across the Land", "Chinese History", "Geography of China", "Cultural Notes", "Sports", "Stamps of New China" and "Chinese Cookery". The "Language Corner" publishes regular lessons in Chinese.

Size: 16-mo

About 76 pages, including 20 pages in full color

Distributed by C.I.B.T.C. to over 140 countries and regions

## BEIJING REVIEW

Beijing Review is China's only foreign-language weekly devoted to news and politics. Established in 1958, it is now published in English, French, Spanish, German and Japanese.

Beijing Review reports on current events in China's political, economic and cultural affairs; carries translations of important Chinese Party and government documents and important statements of Chinese leaders; and expresses China's views on international affairs. Its contents are divided into: "Domestic: Events and Trends", "International: Reports and Comments", "Special Features", and "Articles and Documents", as well as the special columns: "Culture and Science", "The Land and People", "Book Reviews" and "Letters from Readers".

Size: 16-mo

32 pages

Distributed by C.I.B.T.C. to over 150 countries and regions

## PEOPLE'S CHINA

People's China is a comprehensive monthly in Japanese. It was first published fortnightly in English in January 1950, and was followed by a Russian edition (also fortnightly) in January 1951, a Japanese edition (monthly) in June 1953, and Indonesian and French editions (both monthly) in 1958. People's China is currently available only in Japanese.

People's China is intended to promote friendship between the Chinese and Japanese peoples. Its articles cover recent developments in Chinese politics, economics, science, education, culture, art, people's life and other fields. It also publishes short stories and articles providing background knowledge about China. It highlights special subjects through such regular columns as "Literature and Art", "Sports", "People at Various Posts" and "Chinese Products", as well as carrying such special series as "The Silk Road — Yesterday and Today" and "Touring Places of Historical Interest".

Size: 16-mo

128 pages, including 24 of color plates and 16 of black and white photos

Distributed by C.I.B.T.C.

## CHINESE LITERATURE

*Chinese Literature* is a quarterly literary and art magazine. It was first issued in English in October 1951, appearing at irregular intervals. It was published as a quarterly from 1954 to 1958, after which it began to appear as a bimonthly. From 1959 up till 1983, the English edition appeared on a monthly basis. The French edition of *Chinese Literature* first appeared in 1964. Now both its English and French editions are published on a quarterly basis.

*Chinese Literature* introduces a wide range of Chinese literature and art to its foreign readership, stressing works of the contemporary period. In addition, it also prints art and book reviews, articles about writers and artists, and items of cultural news.

Size: 22-mo

The English edition is approximately 240 pages and the French edition approximately 200

Distributed by C.I.B.T.C. to over 120 countries and regions

## EL POPOLA ĈINIO

*El Popola Ĉinio* is a comprehensive monthly in Esperanto edited and published by the China Esperanto League. It was first published as a monthly in May 1950, ceased publication in 1954, and then resumed publication, first as a bimonthly in 1957 and then as a monthly in 1967.

*El Popola Ĉinio* keeps world Esperantists informed of the new achievements in all spheres of China's socialist construction and improvements in the Chinese people's material and cultural well-being, and provides information on Chinese history, geography and culture. It also reports on the activities of Esperantists at home and abroad. Regular columns include "China's Scenic and Historical Sites", "In China's Minority Nationality Areas", "Pages from Chinese History", "Friendship", "Esperanto News" and "New Publications in Esperanto".

Size: 16-mo

About 72 pages, including 8 of color plates and 12 of black and white photos

Distributed by C.I.B.T.C. to over 50 countries and regions

## SOCIAL SCIENCES IN CHINA

Established in 1980, *Social Sciences in China* is a comprehensive philosophical and social science journal sponsored by the Chinese Academy of

Social Sciences. There are two editions: a Chinese bimonthly edition and an English quarterly.

In addition to essays on Marxism-Leninism-Mao Zedong Thought and on special topics in the areas of philosophy and other social sciences, the Chinese edition of *Social Sciences in China* also publishes book reviews and fact-finding reports on economic, cultural and social problems. The English edition of the magazine contains articles selected from the Chinese edition as well as essays written specially for foreign readers.

Size: 16-mo

The Chinese and English editions are approximately 225 pages

Published by the Social Sciences Press

Distributed by C.I.B.T.C.

## SCIENTIA SINICA

*Scientia Sinica* is a comprehensive theoretical magazine of natural science sponsored by the Chinese Academy of Sciences and published in both Chinese and foreign-language editions. The Chinese edition was first published in 1950 and the foreign-language edition in 1952.

*Scientia Sinica* introduces to scientific and technological workers at home and abroad — mainly in the form of dissertations — important achievements made by Chinese scientists in the fields of mathematics, physics, chemistry, astronomy, soil science and biology, and the results of research undertaken in medicine, agriculture and industrial technology. The foreign language edition is published mainly in English, with some articles in French, German and Russian.

Size: 16-mo

The Chinese edition is 96 pages and the foreign language edition 130 pages

Published and distributed by the China Science Press

## KEXUE TONGBAO

*Kexue Tongbao (Science Bulletin)* is a comprehensive academic journal sponsored by the Chinese Academy of Sciences and published in Chinese and foreign languages. The Chinese edition first appeared in 1950 and the foreign language edition in 1966. The Chinese edition became a fortnightly in 1978, while the foreign language edition resumed publication as a monthly in January 1980.

The magazine provides scientific and technological workers at home and abroad with information concerning the achievements of Chinese scientists in the fields of mathematics, physics, chemistry, astronomy, soil science and biology, as well as reports on the results they have obtained in their research work in agriculture, medicine and industrial technology. The foreign language edition is published mainly in English, with some articles in French, German and Russian.

Size: 16-mo

The Chinese edition is 48 pages and the foreign language edition 88 pages

Published and distributed by the China Science Press

## CHINESE MEDICAL JOURNAL

*Chinese Medical Journal* is a comprehensive monthly magazine published by the Chinese Medical Association. It was first published in 1887 in Chinese, with one volume appearing annually. After the founding of the People's Republic of China in 1949, a foreign language edition was added which was published as a bimonthly from 1953 to 1956 and as a monthly from 1957 to 1968. It stopped publication between 1969 and 1974, resuming publication as a bimonthly in 1975 and as a monthly in 1979.

*Chinese Medical Journal* covers progress in Chinese medical research and reports on achievements in medical and health work in China, with the aim of promoting the exchange of scientific knowledge at home and abroad.

## THE LONGEST PAINTED CORRIDOR IN THE WORLD

Located in the northwest of China, the Mogao Grottoes at Dunhuang, Gansu, are one of the greatest treasures of ancient Chinese civilization. The construction of the grottoes began in 366 A.D. and continued for more than a thousand years, spanning ten different dynasties. In this vast complex of caves, there are still 492 which are in a fairly good state of preservation today. They contain some 2,500 painted clay sculptures and 45,000 square meters of painted murals which, if laid end to end, would form the largest painted corridor in the world.

Size: 16-mo

72 pages

Distributed by C.I.B.T.C. to 58 countries and regions

## CHINA'S FOREIGN TRADE

*China's Foreign Trade* is a journal of economics and trade. First published in May 1956, it ceased publication in late 1966 and resumed publication in 1974. It is now a bimonthly, with Chinese, English, French and Spanish editions.

*China's Foreign Trade* keeps world economic and trade circles posted on the achievements in China's socialist modernization program, defines China's policies on foreign trade, introduces China's export commodities and reports on China's foreign trade activities.

Size: 14-mo

68 pages, half in color

Distributed by C.I.B.T.C. to over 150 countries and regions

## WOMEN OF CHINA

An English language magazine devoted to the life of women in China, *Women of China* was first published in 1956 as a quarterly and then as a bimonthly in 1957. It stopped publication in the second half of 1966 and re-sumed publication in March 1979, as a monthly.

*Women of China* acquaints its readers with Chinese women's work, life, social status and contributions to society, marriage and family, as well as the situation in children's education. It also describes Chinese women's participation in revolutionary struggles, the role of celebrated women in Chinese history, and contacts between Chinese women and the women of other countries. Its regular columns include: "Marriage and the Family", "Children", "Letter Box", "Art and Literature", "Events in the Women's Movement", "Historical Stories and Reminiscences" and "Do It Yourself (Chinese cookery or handicrafts)"

Size: 14-mo

48 pages, including 18 in color

Distributed by C.I.B.T.C. to 87 countries and regions

## CHINA SPORTS

*China Sports* is an English language magazine devoted to sports and physical culture in China. It was first published as a quarterly in 1957, appeared as a bimonthly in 1958, and then became a monthly in 1965. It stopped publication in October 1966, and resumed publication as a bimonthly in 1979 and as a monthly in 1980.

*China Sports* keeps world sports enthusiasts informed on

the achievements of Chinese sportsmen and sportswomen in competitions at home and abroad, the lives and work of Chinese coaches and athletes and their interchanges with athletes from other countries, traditional Chinese sports and health-building exercises, as well as Chinese sports history.

Size: 16-mo

36 pages, with color and black and white photographs

Distributed by C.I.B.T.C. to over 60 countries

## CHINA'S SCREEN

China's Screen is a quarterly sponsored by the China Film Distribution and Exhibition Corporation. It was first published in 1958 and stopped publication in the second half of 1966, not resuming publication until the first quarter of 1980. It is now available in Chinese, English and Spanish editions.

China's Screen keeps foreign film distribution corporations and movie enthusiasts informed about the best new films from China and the latest developments in China's film industry. It also covers the interchanges between Chinese film circles and those of other countries and regions.

Size: 16-mo

Approximately 24 pages, consisting mostly of color plates supplemented by brief texts

Distributed by C.I.B.T.C.

## THE WORLD'S FIRST PAPER BOOK

In 1924, a fragment of the novel *History of the Three Kingdoms* was discovered among artifacts unearthed at Shanshan County in the Xinjiang Uygur Autonomous Region. This fragment which contains 801 lines, comprising a total of 1,900 characters, is the world's first book written on paper. The fragment was copied by Chen Shou (233-297) not long after the novel's first appearance. This book fragment is now in a Japanese collection, China merely possessing a photo-offset copy. In 1965, another fragment of this same novel was discovered at the site of a Buddhist pagoda in the ancient city of Yingsha in Turpan in the Xinjiang Uygur Autonomous Region. This latter fragment consists of 40 lines, comprising 570 characters, and recounts events in the life of Emperor Sun Quan of Wu, one of the three kingdoms.

# OFFICIAL HOLIDAYS AND TRADITIONAL FESTIVALS

In China, special holidays are celebrated by particular groups of people. Women throughout the country take a day off on International Women's Day on March 8; young people celebrate National Youth Day on May 4; children are feted on International Children's Day on June 1; servicemen throughout China are honored on National Army's Day on August 1; and the national minorities celebrate their own major national festivals in the minority areas. Besides these special holidays, there are seven days of rest enjoyed by all people in China: three days during the Chinese lunar New Year, also known as the Spring Festival; one on January 1, one on International Labor Day, May 1; and two for China's National Day, October 1. Family-centered as the Chinese are, these holidays are natural occasions for family get-togethers and reunions.

China's long history and diversity of nationalities have given rise to a great many traditional festivals, which are now an important part of the Chinese culture. The most popular of these are as follows:

1) Spring Festival or Chinese lunar New Year. Known also as "passing the year" in Chinese, this is the most important and popular of all Chinese festivals. As early as the Xia dynasty (21st-16th centuries B.C.), the first day of the first month in the lunar calendar was known as the "head of year". But it was not until the Han dynasty (206 B.C.-220 A.D.) that the day became a widely celebrated holiday. After the 1911 Revolution, however, the Gregorian calendar officially replaced the traditional Chinese lunar calendar and the head of year became known as the Spring Festival.

It is important as a family holiday, and on the New Year's Eve (the last day of the twelfth month in the Chinese lunar calendar), the entire family gathers for a sumptuous meal. The principal ritual activity

A Dragon Dance During the Spring Festival

during this festival is known as "New Year's visiting" wherein relatives and friends go to each other's houses and exchange greetings. Spring Festival carnivals vary from place to place, offering lantern and flower displays and the ever-popular lion and dragon dances.

2) Lantern Festival (the 15th day of the first month in the Chinese lunar calendar). The name of this festival is in fact derived from a Tang dynasty (618-907) custom of hanging out lanterns on the night of the festival. The Lantern Festival is also celebrated with round dumplings made of glutinous rice flour and filled with a variety of sweet fillings, known as *yuanxiao* (literally "the night of the first full moon"), which is another name for the festival.

3) Dragon Boat Festival (the fifth day of the fifth month in the Chinese lunar calendar). This festival was established in commemoration of Qu Yuan (c. 340-278 B.C.), a statesman and poet of the Warring States period (475-221 B.C.). An official of the State of Chu, Qu Yuan was thwarted in his ambitions to save his country and threw himself into the Miluo River when the State of Qin conquered Chu. *Zongzi* —

The Rowing Race Along the Miluo River During the 1982 Dragon Boat Festival

glutinous rice dumplings wrapped in bamboo leaves — are served on the festival and dragon boat races are held.

4) Mid-autumn Festival (the 15th day of the eighth month in the Chinese lunar calendar). On this holiday, the Chinese people traditionally eat round "moon cakes" while enjoying a view of the bright, full autumn moon.

5) *Laba* (the eighth day of the 12th month in the Chinese lunar calendar). *Laba* was originally a religious holiday in celebration of Sakyamuni's attainment of Buddhahood. Buddhists of the Han nationality would make an offering to the Buddha of a steamed pudding made of rice and fruit called "*Laba* pudding". The holiday has long been secularized and the pudding remains very popular.

China's minority nationalities celebrate a number of traditional festivals, including their own New Years.

1) "Nadam" Fair — a traditional Mongolian gathering held once a year at the regional, league and banner levels. In Mongolian "Nadam" means "recreation" or "games". The "Nadam" Fair features wrestling matches, horseraces, archery contests and singing and dancing performances.

2) Fruit-Expecting Festival — an annual Tibetan festival celebrated in anticipation of the harvest. Beginning on August 1, it lasts for an unfixed number of days, and includes horseracing, Tibetan drama, singing, dancing and bartering.

3) April 8th Festival — a major event in the Miao communities surrounding the city of Guiyang in Guizhou Province believed to have originated in the Ming dynasty (1368-1644). On the day of the festival, Miao youth dressed in their holiday best gather at a fountain at the center of Guiyang in commemoration of Yanu, the Miao national hero. More recently it has become a multinational gathering.

4) Song Fair (or Songstress Festival). This is a carnival devoted to singing and dancing held among the Zhuang communities in the Guangxi Zhuang Autonomous Region. It is usually held on the 15th day of the first month, the eighth day of the third and fourth months and the 12th day of the fifth month in the Chinese lunar calendar.

5) Torch Festival — a popular festival among the Yi and Bai communities in Yunnan and parts of Sichuan. In the evening, the entire community

makes rounds of the fields carrying lighted torches, and then feast and drink to the accompaniment of singing and dancing. Beginning on the 24th day of the sixth month in the Chinese lunar calendar, it may last for one to three successive nights.

6) Third Moon Fair (or Goddess of Mercy Festival) celebrated by the Bai communities in Yunnan and neighboring provinces. From the 15th to the 20th of the third month in the Chinese lunar calendar, people of all nationalities will gather at Dali for horseraces, archery competitions, singing, dancing and bartering.

7) Third Day of the Third Month — a festival held among Li minority communities living on Hainan Island. On this day, people gather in anticipation of the upcoming harvest, and young men and women have an opportunity to meet their potential spouses.

8) "Danu" Festival (the 29th day of the fifth month in the Chinese lunar calendar). The major holiday of the Yao people, it is celebrated at harvest time.

## THE FIRST SEISMOGRAPH IN THE WORLD

Violent earthquakes occurred several times in China between 95 and 125 A.D. The quakes prompted Zhang Heng (78-139), a Chinese scientist, to invent the first seismograph in the world in 132.

The seismograph was like an octagonal wine vessel with eight metal dragons, each with a small bronze ball in the mouth, beneath which crouched eight bronze toads with open mouths facing upwards. A bronze shaft which narrowed towards the bottom stood in the center of the seismograph. When an earthquake occurred, the shaft would topple over in the direction of the earthquake's epicenter, and a dragon's mouth would open and let the bronze ball plop into the toad's mouth below, letting people know the approximate area where the earthquake was taking place.

In 138, the seismograph in Luoyang, 500 kilometers from the epicenter, recorded an earthquake happening in southeastern Gansu Province. Nothing like this seismograph appeared in Europe until 1,700 years later.

# THE CHINESE LANGUAGE AND ITS DIALECTS

Chinese language, also known as *hanyu,* usually refers to the standard language and its various dialects used by the Han nationality. which makes up 93.3 percent of China's population. Most of the minority nationalities have their own languages. Both numerically and in the extent of its distribution, Chinese is the most important language in China. Chinese is not only the lingua franca of China but also one of the five official working languages of the United Nations. It is also one of the richest and most highly developed languages in the world.

Chinese is also spoken by many overseas Chinese: it is the common language of more than ten million overseas Chinese and persons of Chinese descent in Southeast Asia alone. At present, more than one billion people speak Chinese as their mother tongue, or approximately one-fifth of the world's population.

A written form of the language was developed as early as 6,000 years ago. From the point of view of its origin, it belongs to the Sino-Tibetan language family.

Chinese subdivides into the following dialects, which in their spoken form are mutually unintelligible:

1. Northern dialect (*beifanghua*): This is the most widely spoken dialect in China, and forms the basis of *putonghua* ("common speech", sometimes called Mandarin), the official language of the People's Republic of China and the lingua franca of the Han nationality. Its use is centered in the Huanghe River valley, and is spoken throughout the provinces of the northeast, the central part of the Changjiang River basin, and the provinces of the southwest. The northern dialect is spoken by more than 70 percent of the Chinese population.

2. Wu dialect, spoken in the Shanghai region, southeastern Jiangsu Province and most of Zhejiang Province.

3. Xiang dialect, spoken by the inhabitants of Hunan Province (with the exception of the northwestern area).

4. Gan dialect, spoken throughout Jiangxi Province (with the exception of the area bordering the Changjiang River and the southern area), and in southeastern Hubei Province.

5. Kejia (Hakka) dialect, spoken in parts of Guangdong, Guangxi, Fujian and Jiangxi provinces.

6. Northern Min dialect, spoken in parts of northern Fujian and Taiwan provinces.

7. Southern Min dialect, spoken throughout southern Fujian Province as well as in the Chaozhou and Shantou districts of Guangdong Province, in parts of Hainan Island, and throughout most of Taiwan Province. Southern Min is also spoken by many overseas Chinese.

8. Yue dialect (Cantonese), spoken throughout central and southwestern Guangdong Province as well as in the southeastern part of the Guangxi Zhuang Autonomous Region. Cantonese is also spoken by many overseas Chinese.

## THE WORLD'S FIRST FULLY SUCCESSFUL LIMB REPLANTING OPERATION

In January 1963, a team of surgeons at the Shanghai No. 6 People's Hospital performed surgery on a 27-year-old young worker whose forearm had been completely severed from his body. Led by Chen Zhongwei, the team of surgeons drew up a well-conceived plan and performed a successful limb replanting operation. The patient rapidly recovered use of his replanted limb, such that six months after the operation he could write, play ping-pong and carry objects not heavier than six kilograms. At the 20th meeting of the International Surgery Conference in Rome in September 1962, the participants agreed that this was the first instance of a limb replanting operation which had obtained entirely satisfactory results.

# THE CHINESE WRITTEN LANGUAGE

The Chinese language is written in the form of symbols usually known as characters. They have an age-old history and a complex structure, and are extremely rich in variety. Originating approximately 6,000 years ago, they constitute one of the world's earlist written languages.

It is estimated that Chinese characters were first systematized in the early Xia dynasty (c. 21st-16th centuries B.C.), but some experts believe that the date was even earlier. The earliest characters are the oracle bone inscriptions of the later Shang dynasty (c. 16th-11th centuries B.C.), which were carved on tortoise shells and animal bones for use in divination, and the later inscriptions found on bronze ritual vessels.

Modern Chinese characters evolved directly from those found on these early inscriptions. Pictographs resembling the objects they represent gradually evolved into characters capable of expressing more abstract concepts, and elaborate characters gradually became simplified. This process of evolution culminated in modern logophonetic characters, with one element or group of elements indicating meaning and the other elements indicating sound. At present, each character in the Chinese language represents a single word. The large majority are logophonetic, although some pictographic and ideographic elements have been retained. The *Kangxi Dictionary* (1716) contains more than 40 000 characters, but of these only between five and eight thousand are in common use today.

Beginning with the oracle bone characters, the written forms of Chinese characters have gone through three major developmental phases. In the first phase, the characters progressed from primitive pictographs to linear designs. In the second phase, the characters became more linear still, representing an advance in simplification and standardization over the earlier characters. The script representative of this phase is known as the *dazhuan*, or "great seal".

With the unification of China in 221 B.C. under the Qin dynasty, a new style of characters called *xiaozhuan*, or "lesser seal", was promulgated as the standard form of the written language. In this final developmental phase, Chinese characters were first written with a brush, which had a significant impact on their written forms.

Chinese characters are basically square in shape, and are often described as "square characters" in Chinese. The 11 different basic brush strokes used — in various combinations and permutations — to write Chinese characters are as follows:

1. dot ╲
2. horizontal stroke ━
3. perpendicular stroke │
4. downstroke to the left ╱
5. downstroke to the right ╲
6. short rising stroke ╱
7. Horizontal stroke with a short downward hook ┑
8. perpendicular stroke with an upward hook to the left ┛
9. oblique downward stroke with an upward hook to the right ╲
10. horizontal dash with an abrupt downward stroke ┑
11. perpendicular downward stroke with a curve to the right ╰

The six evolutionary stages in the development of Chinese characters are:

1.      2.      3.      4.      5.      6.

(sun) (moon) (vehicle) (horse)

1. Oracle Bone Characters (*jiaguwen*); 2. Bronze Vessel Characters (*jinwen*); 3. Lesser Seal Characters (*xiaozhuan*); 4. Official Script (*lishu*); 5. Regular Script (*kaishu*); and 6. Semi-cursive Script (*xingshu*).

214

A study undertaken by the Publications Bureau of the Ministry of Culture of the People's Republic of China revealed that in a sample of 20 million characters selected from contemporary books and magazines only 6,335 different characters were used. Among these, 2,400 appeared frequently, 1,770 appeared infrequently and 2,165 were used only rarely.

## REFORM OF CHINESE WRITTEN LANGUAGE

Chinese characters have made a great and permanent contribution to world culture, but they are complex in form and vast in number, making the written Chinese language difficult and time-consuming to master. It is important, then, for China to reform its written language and adopt a system of romanization or phoneticization to facilitate international communication.

The simplification of Chinese characters undertaken by the government of the People's Republic since 1949 follows ineluctable historical trends and has been instrumental in popularizing education in China and making the written language faster and easier to learn. In 1964, the Chinese government approved of a "Draft Proposal Concerning the Simplification of Chinese Characters" prepared by the Committee on the Reform of the Written Language. The benefits of these new simplified characters became obvious as soon as they were put into circulation.

Phonetic Scripts (Romanized Characters) of the Chinese language were adopted in 1958. They are now widely used as a help to beginner-learners of the language and in international communication.

A number of new simplified characters compared with their traditional unsimplified forms are given below:

| some | 几 | 幾 |
| cloud | 云 | 雲 |
| orchid | 兰 | 蘭 |
| vast | 广 | 廣 |
| air | 气 | 氣 |
| wind | 风 | 風 |
| hall | 厅 | 廳 |
| for | 为 | 爲 |
| dragon | 龙 | 龍 |
| ugly | 丑 | 醜 |
| old | 旧 | 舊 |

# CHINA'S CURRENCY

December 1, 1948 marked the founding of the People's Bank of China and the first issuance of *renminbi* (people's currency), the currency of China. However, the *renminbi* used today was first issued on March 1, 1955. The symbol for *renminbi* is "¥", which is derived from the first letter of the romanized spelling of *yuan*, the principal unit of the currency. The *yuan* is divided into 100 *fen*; 10 *fen* equal 1 *jiao* (or *mao*). The face values of the notes as follows: ¥10, ¥5, ¥2, ¥1, 5 *jiao*, 2 *jiao*, 1 *jiao*, 5 *fen*, 2 *fen* and 1 *fen*. There are also coins of 5 *fen*, 2 *fen* and 1 *fen*.

The official exchange quotations rate in RMB *yuan* on January 15, 1984 is on the oppsite page.

## EXCHANGE QUOTATIONS RATE IN RMB YUAN
### (January 15, 1984)

| Currency | | Per | Buying | Selling |
|---|---|---|---|---|
| Australia | $ | 100 | 184.06 | 184.98 |
| Austria | Sch | 100 | 10.18 | 10.24 |
| Belgium | Fr | 10,000 | (c)353.99 | 355.77 |
| | | | (f)347.63 | 349.37 |
| Canada | $ | 100 | 162.88 | 163.70 |
| Denmark | Kr | 100 | 20.05 | 20.15 |
| F.R.G. | Dm | 100 | 72.74 | 73.10 |
| Finland | Mk | 100 | 33.80 | 33.96 |
| France | Fr | 100 | 23.62 | 23.76 |
| Ghana | Cedi | 100 | 6.72 | 6.76 |
| Iran | Rial | 10,000 | 229.71 | 230.87 |
| Italy | Lira | 10,000 | 11.87 | 11.93 |
| Japan | Yen | 100,000 | 869.39 | 873.75 |
| Holland | G | 100 | 64.69 | 65.01 |
| Norway | Kr | 100 | 25.72 | 25.84 |
| Pakistan | Rs | 100 | 15.04 | 15.12 |
| Sierra Leone | Le | 100 | 79.15 | 79.55 |
| Singapore | $ | 100 | 95.02 | 95.50 |
| Sweden | Kr | 100 | 24.91 | 25.03 |
| Swiss | Fr | 100 | 90.87 | 91.33 |
| U.K. | £ | 100 | 287.68 | 289.12 |
| USA | $ | 100 | 203.59 | 204.61 |
| Hongkong | $ | 100 | 26.11 | 26.25 |

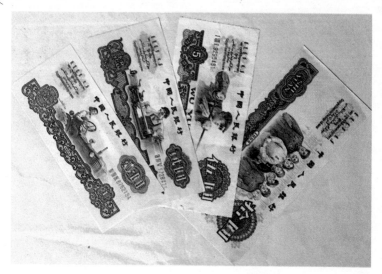

Notes of Ten Yuan, Five Yuan, Two Yuan and One Yuan

The Reverse Sides of the Above Notes

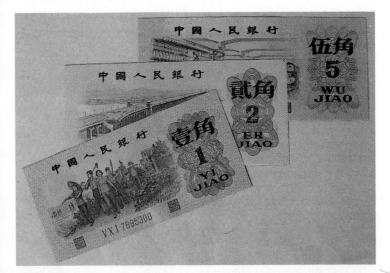

Notes of Five Jiao, Two Jiao and
One Jiao

The Reverse Sides of the Above
Notes

In the Chinese language, many written characters with meaning related to value, wealth, finance and trade contain the element 贝 a pictograph of a cowrie shell. From this it can easily be inferred that the earliest currency used in China was cowrie shells, a fact demonstrated by the excavation of such shells from a tomb in the Yin ruins dating from the Shang dynasty (16th-11th centuries B.C.) in Anyang County, Henan Province. From this discovery, it can be concluded that shell currency was first used in China from the 17th to 16th centuries B.C. (Illus. 1). The earliest metal currency discovered to date was a bronze cowrie (Illus. 2) dating from the 14th to 11th centuries B.C. Subsequently, a wide variety of bronze coins, knife coins and other metal coins came into use. When Qin Shi Huang, the first emperor of the Qin dynasty, unified China in 221 B.C., he standardized the currency and abolished shell coins, bronze coins and knife coins, replacing them with

Illus. 3

Illus. 4

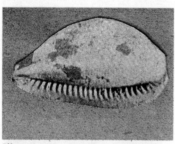

Illus. 1

Illus. 2

round bronze coins with a square hole in the middle (Illus. 3-4). Such coins, in various sizes and materials, served as the main form of metal currency for the ensuing 20 centuries up to the Republican period in the early 20th century.

In addition to bronze coins, China's early currency was also made of gold, silver and iron. The earliest gold coins unearthed to date were those circulated in the state of Chu (770-221 B.C.), known as *ying-yuan*. "Ying" was the capital of Chu; "yuan" a measure of weight (Illus. 5). A second

Illus. 6

vented in China. The earliest paper money in China, and perhaps in the world, was the *jiaozi* (Illus. 7), dating from the Northern Song dynasty (960-1127 A.D.). *Jiaozi* (literal-

Illus. 7

Illus. 5

type was the 5-*zhu* (a unit of weight) coins (Illus. 6) from the Western Han dynasty (140-87 B.C.).

Paper money was first inly "notes of exchange") could be exchanged for metal currency or used as cash in trade. In 1107 the name of the currency was changed from *jiaozi* to *qianyin* (literally "cash tender"). *Qianyin* notes were printed with six separate wooden blocks in three colors — black, blue and red — and marked the beginning of color printing in China. In 1260, Kublai Khan, the first emperor of the Yuan dynasty (1271-1368), issued the paper currency known as *zhongtongchao* (Illus. 8). Marco Polo, who was employed in the Yuan court at this time, took a great interest in this paper currency and wrote about it in his famous travelogue.

Illus. 8

# THE GREAT WALL

## — The Only Man-Made Object Visible from the Moon

When they landed on the moon in 1969, the two American astronauts were reportedly surprised to discover the only traces of human civilization on earth visible to the naked eye was the Great Wall of China. Starting from Shanhaiguan Pass at the Bohai Sea and winding its way through rough mountainous terrain to Jiayuguan Pass, a point deep in Central Asia, the Great Wall covers a total distance of 6,700 kilometers, and stands as the largest construction project ever carried out.

Parts of the Wall date from the Warring States Period (475-221 B.C.), when each state built fortified walls along its border to ward off possible invasions from its hostile neighbors. In 214 B.C., after emperor Qin Shi Huang conquered the other six states and finally succeeded in unifying China, he reinforced the walls along the northern borders of the original Qin, Yan and Zhao states and had them connected into one defense system.

The Great Wall was substantially rebuilt in later times. The present shape of the Great Wall owes much to the repeated large-scale expansion and rebuilding carried out during the Ming dynasty (1368-1644).

# PRICE INDICES

PRICE INDICES (1951-1981)  1950 = 100

| Year | Overall index of retail prices | Overall index of urban cost of living | Overall index of ex-factory prices of industrial products | Overall index of purchase prices for farm produce and sideline production | Overall index of retail list prices of rural industrial products | Index of price parity between industrial and agricultural products (overall index of purchase prices for farm produce and sideline production as 100) |
|------|------|------|------|------|------|------|
| 1951 | 112.2 | 112.5 | 113.9 | 119.6 | 110.2 | 92.1 |
| 1952 | 111.8 | 115.5 | 113.2 | 121.6 | 109.7 | 90.2 |
| 1953 | 115.6 | 121.4 | 109.5 | 132.5 | 108.2 | 81.7 |
| 1954 | 118.3 | 123.1 | 107.8 | 136.7 | 110.3 | 80.7 |
| 1955 | 119.5 | 123.5 | 106.4 | 135.1 | 111.9 | 82.8 |
| 1956 | 119.5 | 123.4 | 98.5 | 139.2 | 110.8 | 79.6 |
| 1957 | 121.3 | 126.6 | 98.7 | 146.2 | 112.1 | 76.7 |
| 1958 | 121.6 | 125.2 | 98.1 | 149.4 | 111.4 | 74.6 |
| 1959 | 122.7 | 125.6 | 98.7 | 152.1 | 112.4 | 73.9 |
| 1960 | 126.5 | 128.8 | 98.0 | 157.4 | 115.5 | 73.4 |
| 1961 | 147.0 | 149.6 | 102.9 | 201.4 | 121.2 | 60.2 |
| 1962 | 152.6 | 155.3 | 106.9 | 200.1 | 126.6 | 63.3 |
| 1963 | 143.6 | 146.1 | 106.3 | 194.4 | 125.3 | 64.5 |
| 1964 | 138.3 | 140.7 | 104.2 | 189.5 | 122.9 | 64.9 |
| 1965 | 134.6 | 139.0 | 99.3 | 187.9 | 118.4 | 63.0 |
| 1966 | 134.2 | 137.3 | 95.1 | 195.8 | 115.0 | 58.7 |
| 1967 | 133.2 | 136.4 | 93.9 | 195.5 | 114.1 | 58.4 |
| 1968 | 133.3 | 136.5 | 91.9 | 195.2 | 113.8 | 58.3 |
| 1969 | 131.8 | 137.8 | 88.8 | 194.9 | 112.1 | 57.5 |
| 1970 | 131.5 | 137.8 | 84.9 | 195.1 | 111.9 | 57.4 |
| 1971 | 130.5 | 137.7 | 84.4 | 198.3 | 110.2 | 55.6 |
| 1972 | 130.2 | 137.9 | 83.9 | 201.1 | 109.6 | 54.5 |
| 1973 | 131.0 | 138.0 | 83.5 | 202.8 | 109.6 | 54.0 |
| 1974 | 131.7 | 138.9 | 82.7 | 204.5 | 109.6 | 53.6 |
| 1975 | 131.9 | 139.5 | 82.4 | 208.7 | 109.6 | 52.5 |
| 1976 | 132.3 | 139.9 | 82.2 | 209.7 | 109.7 | 52.3 |
| 1977 | 135.0 | 143.7 | 81.4 | 209.2 | 109.8 | 52.5 |
| 1978 | 135.9 | 144.7 | 81.6 | 217.4 | 109.8 | 50.5 |
| 1979 | 138.6 | 147.4 | 82.9 | 265.5 | 109.9 | 41.4 |
| 1980 | 146.9 | 158.5 | 83.4 | 284.4 | 110.8 | 39.0 |
| 1981 | 150.4 | 162.5 | 83.6 | 301.2 | 111.9 | 37.2 |

## 1981 PRICE INDICES COMPARED WITH PREVIOUS YEARS

| Base period | Overall index of retail prices | Overall index of urban cost of living | Overall index of purchase prices for farm produce and sideline production | Overall index of retail list prices of rural industrial products | Index of price parity between industrial and agricultural products (overall index of purchase prices for farm produce and sideline production as 100) |
|---|---|---|---|---|---|
| Average prices of 1930-1936 as 100 | 351.2 | | 567.8 | 283.4 | 49.9 |
| 1950 prices as 100 | 150.4 | 162.5 | 301.2 | 111.9 | 37.2 |
| 1952 prices as 100 | 134.6 | 140.6 | 247.7 | 102.0 | 41.2 |
| 1957 prices as 100 | 124.0 | 128.3 | 206.0 | 99.8 | 48.4 |
| 1962 prices as 100 | 98.6 | 104.7 | 150.5 | 88.4 | 58.7 |
| 1965 prices as 100 | 111.7 | 116.9 | 160.3 | 94.5 | 59.0 |
| 1970 prices as 100 | 114.4 | 117.9 | 154.4 | 100.0 | 64.8 |
| 1975 prices as 100 | 114.1 | 116.4 | 144.3 | 102.1 | 70.8 |
| 1980 prices as 100 | 102.4 | 102.5 | 105.9 | 101.0 | 95.4 |

**Note:** In these two lists, the overall indices of retail prices and the urban cost of living include the indices of list prices, negotiated prices and market prices. The overall index of purchase prices for farm produce and sideline production includes the indices of list prices, negotiated prices and higher prices for purchases beyond quotas.

225

## OVERALL INDICES OF RETAIL PRICES
## IN DIFFERENT REGIONS IN 1981

1980 = 100

| Region | Provincial (city, district) average | Urban | Rural |
|---|---|---|---|
| National average | 102.4 | 102.7 | 102.1 |
| Beijing | 101.4 | 101.4 | |
| Tianjin | 101.5 | 101.5 | |
| Hebei | 102.1 | 103.4 | 101.6 |
| Shanxi | 102.3 | 103.2 | 101.6 |
| Inner Mongolia | 101.8 | 101.6 | 102.1 |
| Liaoning | 101.6 | 102.1 | 100.9 |
| Jilin | 101.7 | 101.8 | 101.2 |
| Heilongjiang | 102.1 | 102.3 | 101.9 |
| Shanghai | 101.5 | 101.5 | |
| Jiangsu | 101.6 | 102.4 | 101.3 |
| Zhejiang | 101.5 | 101.6 | 101.4 |
| Anhui | 101.7 | 103.5 | 100.9 |
| Fujian | 103.4 | 103.7 | 102.6 |
| Jiangxi | 104.6 | 104.0 | 105.2 |
| Shandong | 101.8 | 101.9 | 101.4 |
| Henan | 101.6 | 102.6 | 100.8 |
| Hubei | 101.4 | 102.2 | 100.6 |
| Hunan | 100.9 | 101.8 | 100.5 |
| Guangdong | 109.3 | 106.9 | 110.3 |
| Guangxi | 101.7 | 103.0 | 100.5 |
| Sichuan | 101.8 | 102.8 | 101.0 |
| Guizhou | 102.3 | 103.2 | 101.5 |
| Yunnan | 101.2 | 100.8 | 101.4 |
| Shaanxi | 103.0 | 104.1 | 101.7 |
| Gansu | 102.0 | 102.6 | 101.7 |
| Qinghai | 101.4 | 101.4 | 101.3 |
| Ningxia | 102.0 | 102.0 | 101.8 |
| Xinjiang | 101.6 | 102.6 | 101.2 |

**Note:** Indices include list prices, negotiated prices and market prices.

# COMPOSITE AVERAGE RETAIL PRICES OF PRINCIPAL INDUSTRIAL AND AGRICULTURAL PRODUCTS

Unit:  RMB yuan

| Name of product | Unit | 1981 | 1980 |
|---|---|---|---|
| Grain | metric ton | 337.1 | 307.5 |
| Edible vegetable oil | " | 1,967.4 | 1,713.5 |
| Pork | 100 kgs | 210.8 | 202.2 |
| Beef | " | 188.4 | 176.0 |
| Mutton | " | 170.2 | 164.8 |
| Poultry | 100 | 262.4 | 251.6 |
| Eggs | 100 kgs | 215.2 | 207.8 |
| Aquatic products | metric ton | 1,349.3 | 1,263.3 |
| Vegetables | " | 134.0 | 122.0 |
| Sugar | " | 1,491.6 | 1,477.4 |
| Cigarettes | 10,000 | 738.1 | 672.6 |
| Alcoholic beverages | metric ton | 2,230.6 | 2,038.1 |
| Table salt | " | 287.1 | 289.7 |
| Tea | 100 kgs | 854.4 | 795.2 |
| Cotton cloth | meter | 1.59 | 1.58 |
| Cotton synthetic blend fabric | " | 3.45 | |
| Cotton polyester fabric | " | 4.67 | 5.35 |
| Synthetic fabric | " | 3.97 | |
| Woollen piece goods | " | 18.58 | 18.10 |
| Silk | " | 3.53 | 3.47 |
| Towels | 100 pieces | 79.6 | 76.8 |
| Socks | 100 pairs | 163.5 | 172.6 |
| Undershirts | 100 pieces | 161.3 | 159.7 |
| Cotton underwear | " | 406.7 | 404.0 |
| Thermal underwear | " | 568.3 | 562.7 |
| Knitting wool | 100 kgs | 3,223.8 | 3,223.8 |
| Cotton for wadding | " | 203.6 | 203.6 |
| Leather shoes | 100 pairs | 1,334.3 | 1,194.9 |

| Name of product | Unit | 1981 | 1980 |
|---|---|---|---|
| Rubber shoes | 100 pairs | 485.0 | 476.8 |
| Cotton shoes | " | 368.6 | 363.3 |
| Plastic shoes | " | 264.6 | 263.8 |
| Matches | 1,000 boxes | 20.6 | 20.1 |
| Soap | 160 bars | 26.1 | 26.0 |
| Toilet soap | 100 pieces | 44.2 | 44.3 |
| Detergent | 100 kgs | 147.4 | 144.4 |
| Thermos bottles | 100 | 444.4 | 425.0 |
| Aluminium pots | " | 605.5 | 624.6 |
| Enamel mugs | " | 88.5 | 90.7 |
| Enamel washbasins | " | 297.9 | 293.1 |
| Electric torches | " | 185.2 | 175.8 |
| Fountain pens | " | 775.5 | 718.1 |
| Iridium-point fountain pens | " | 162.4 | 160.3 |
| Sewing machines | piece | 148.6 | 147.2 |
| Bicycles | " | 163.7 | 161.2 |
| Watches | " | 113.5 | 122.8 |
| Clocks | " | 23.1 | 21.1 |
| Tube radios | " | 114.6 | 111.2 |
| Transistor radios | " | 41.4 | 40.7 |
| Television sets | " | 502.6 | 551.7 |
| Machine-made paper | metric ton | 1,873.4 | 1,865.4 |
| Kerosene | " | 701.5 | 701.3 |
| Coal | " | 32.6 | 31.4 |
| Chemical fertilizers | " | 242.5 | 237.1 |
| Motors for agricultural use | horsepower | 89.1 | 90.3 |
| Timber | cubic meter | 197.4 | 149.3 |

**Note:** Composite average retail prices are calculated by dividing quantity of retail goods sold by the retail prices of each product, for variation in price and quality with adjustments.

# A LIST OF COUNTRIES WHICH HAVE DIPLOMATIC RELATIONS WITH CHINA

(in chronological order)

| | Name of Country | Date of Establishment of Relations | Location |
|---|---|---|---|
| 1) | The Union of Soviet Socialist Republics | Oct. 3, 1949 | Europe |
| 2) | The People's Republic of Bulgaria | Oct. 4, 1949 | Europe |
| 3) | The Socialist Republic of Romania | Oct. 5, 1949 | Europe |
| 4) | The Hungarian People's Republic | Oct. 6, 1949 | Europe |
| 5) | The Democratic People's Republic of Korea | Oct. 6, 1949 | Asia |
| 6) | The Czechoslovak Socialist Republic | Oct. 6, 1949 | Europe |
| 7) | The People's Republic of Poland | Oct. 7, 1949 | Europe |
| 8) | The People's Republic of Mongolia | Oct. 16, 1949 | Asia |
| 9) | The German Democratic Republic | Oct. 27, 1949 | Europe |
| 10) | The People's Socialist Republic of Albania | Nov. 23, 1949 | Europe |
| 11) | The Socialist Republic of Viet Nam | Jan. 18, 1950 | Asia |
| 12) | The Republic of India | April 1, 1950 | Asia |
| 13) | The Kingdom of Sweden | May 9, 1950 | Europe |

| | Name of Country | Date of Estab- lishment of Relations | Location |
|---|---|---|---|
| 14) | The Kingdom of Denmark | May 11, 1950 | Europe |
| 15) | The Socialist Republic of the Union of Burma | June 8, 1950 | Asia |
| 16) | The Swiss Confederation | Sept. 14, 1950 | Europe |
| 17) | The Republic of Finland | Oct. 28, 1950 | Europe |
| 18) | The Islamic Republic of Pakistan | May 21, 1951 | Asia |
| 19) | The Kingdom of Norway | Oct. 5, 1954 | Europe |
| 20) | The Socialist Federal Republic of Yugoslavia | Jan. 2, 1955 | Europe |
| 21) | The Democratic Republic of Afghanistan | Jan. 20, 1955 | Asia |
| 22) | The Kingdom of Nepal | Aug. 1, 1955 | Asia |
| 23) | The Arab Republic of Egypt | May 30, 1956 | Africa |
| 24) | The Arab Republic of Syria | Aug. 1, 1956 | Asia |
| 25) | The Arab Republic of Yemen | Sept. 24, 1956 | Asia |
| 26) | The Democratic Socialist Republic of Sri Lanka | Feb. 7, 1957 | Asia |
| 27) | Democratic Kampuchea | July 19, 1958 | Asia |
| 28) | The Republic of Iraq | Aug. 20, 1958 | Asia |
| 29) | The Kingdom of Morocco | Nov. 1, 1958 | Africa |
| 30) | The Democratic People's Republic of Algeria | Dec. 20, 1958 | Africa |
| 31) | The Democratic Republic of the Sudan | Feb. 4, 1959 | Africa |
| 32) | The People's Revolutionary Republic of Guinea | Oct. 4, 1959 | Africa |
| 33) | The Republic of Ghana | July 5, 1960 | Africa |
| 34) | The Republic of Cuba | Sept. 28, 1960 | Latin Americ. |

| | Name of Country | Date of Establishment of Relations | Location |
|---|---|---|---|
| 35) | The Republic of Mali | Oct. 25, 1960 | Africa |
| 36) | The Somali Democratic Republic | Dec. 14, 1960 | Africa |
| 37) | The Republic of Zaire | Feb. 20, 1961 | Africa |
| 38) | The People's Democratic Republic of Laos | April 25, 1961 | Asia |
| 39) | The Republic of Uganda | Oct. 18, 1962 | Africa |
| 40) | The Republic of Kenya | Dec. 14, 1963 | Africa |
| 41) | The Republic of Burundi | Dec. 21, 1963 | Africa |
| 42) | The Republic of Tunisia | Jan. 10, 1964 | Africa |
| 43) | The French Republic | Jan. 27, 1964 | Europe |
| 44) | The People's Republic of the Congo | Feb. 22, 1964 | Africa |
| 45) | The United Republic of Tanzania | April 26, 1964 | Africa |
| 46) | The Republic of Central Africa | Sept. 29, 1964 | Africa |
| 47) | The Republic of Zambia | Oct. 29, 1964 | Africa |
| 48) | The People's Republic of Benin | Nov. 12, 1964 | Africa |
| 49) | The Islamic Republic of Mauritania | July 19, 1965 | Africa |
| 50) | The People's Democratic Republic of Yemen | Jan. 31, 1968 | Asia |
| 51) | Canada | Oct. 13, 1970 | North America |
| 52) | The Republic of Equatorial Guinea | Oct. 15, 1970 | Africa |
| 53) | The Italian Republic | Nov. 6, 1970 | Europe |
| 54) | The Socialist Ethiopia | Nov. 24, 1970 | Africa |
| 55) | The Republic of Chile | Dec. 15, 1970 | Latin America |
| 56) | The Federal Republic of Nigeria | Feb. 10, 1971 | Africa |

| Name of Country | Date of Establishment of Relations | Location |
|---|---|---|
| 57) The State of Kuwait | March 22, 1971 | Asia |
| 58) The United Republic of Cameroon | March 26, 1971 | Africa |
| 59) The Republic of San Marino | May 6, 1971 | Europe |
| 60) The Republic of Austria | May 28, 1971 | Europe |
| 61) The Republic of Sierra Leone | July 29, 1971 | Africa |
| 62) The Republic of Turkey | Aug. 4, 1971 | Asia |
| 63) The Islamic Republic of Iran | Aug. 16, 1971 | Asia |
| 64) The Kingdom of Belgium | Oct. 25, 1971 | Europe |
| 65) The Republic of Peru | Nov. 2, 1971 | Latin America |
| 66) The Lebanese Republic | Nov. 9, 1971 | Asia |
| 67) The Republic of Rwanda | Nov. 12, 1971 | Africa |
| 68) The Republic of Senegal | Dec. 7, 1971 | Africa |
| 69) The Republic of Iceland | Dec. 8, 1971 | Europe |
| 70) The Republic of Cyprus | Dec. 14, 1971 | Asia |
| 71) The Republic of Malta | Jan. 31, 1972 | Europe |
| 72) The Union States of Mexico | Feb. 14, 1972 | Latin America |
| 73) The Argentine Republic | Feb. 19, 1972 | Latin America |
| 74) The United Kingdom of Great Britain and Northern Ireland | March 13, 1972 | Europe |
| 75) Mauritius | April 15, 1972 | Africa |
| 76) The Kingdom of the Netherlands | May 18, 1972 | Europe |
| 77) The Hellenic Republic | June 5, 1972 | Europe |
| 78) The Co-operative Republic of Guyana | June 27, 1972 | Latin America |
| 79) The Republic of Togo | Sept. 19, 1972 | Africa |
| 80) Japan | Sept. 29, 1972 | Asia |

| | Name of Country | Date of Establishment of Relations | Location |
|---|---|---|---|
| 81) | The Federal Republic of Germany | Oct. 11, 1972 | Europe |
| 82) | The Republic of Maldives | Oct. 14, 1972 | Asia |
| 83) | The Democratic Republic of Madagascar | Nov. 6, 1972 | Africa |
| 84) | The Grand Duchy of Luxemburg | Nov. 16, 1972 | Europe |
| 85) | Jamaica | Nov. 21, 1972 | Latin America |
| 86) | The Republic of Chad | Nov. 28, 1972 | Africa |
| 87) | The Commonwealth of Australia | Dec. 21, 1972 | Oceania |
| 88) | New Zealand | Dec. 22, 1972 | Oceania |
| 89) | The Spanish State | March 9, 1973 | Europe |
| 90) | The Burkina-Faso | Sept. 15, 1973 | Africa |
| 91) | The Republic of Guinea-Bissau | March 15, 1974 | Africa |
| 92) | The Republic of Gabon | April 20, 1974 | Africa |
| 93) | Federation of Malaysia | May 31, 1974 | Asia |
| 94) | The Republic of Trinidad and Tobago | June 20, 1974 | Latin America |
| 95) | The Republic of Venezuela | June 28, 1974 | Latin America |
| 96) | The Republic of Niger | July 20, 1974 | Africa |
| 97) | The Federative Republic of Brazil | Aug. 15, 1974 | Latin America |
| 98) | The Republic of the Gambia | Dec. 14, 1974 | Africa |
| 99) | The Republic of Botswana | Jan. 6, 1975 | Africa |
| 100) | The Republic of the Philippines | June 9, 1975 | Asia |
| 101) | The People's Republic of Mozambique | June 25, 1975 | Africa |
| 102) | The Kingdom of Thailand | July 1, 1975 | Asia |

| | Name of Country | Date of Estab-lishment of Relations | Location |
|---|---|---|---|
| 103) | The Democratic Republic of Sao Tome and Principe | July 12, 1975 | Africa |
| 104) | The People's Republic of Bangladesh | Oct. 4, 1975 | Asia |
| 105) | Fiji | Nov. 5, 1975 | Oceania |
| 106) | Western Samoa | Nov. 6, 1975 | Oceania |
| 107) | The Islamic Federal Republic of Comoros | Nov. 13, 1975 | Africa |
| 108) | The Republic of Cape Verde | April 25, 1976 | Africa |
| 109) | The Republic of Surinam | May 28, 1976 | Latin America |
| 110) | The Republic of Seychelles | June 30, 1976 | Africa |
| 111) | Papua New Guinea | Oct. 12, 1976 | Oceania |
| 112) | The Republic of Liberia | Feb. 17, 1977 | Africa |
| 113) | The Hashemite Kingdom of Jordan | April 7, 1977 | Asia |
| 114) | Barbados | May 30, 1977 | Latin America |
| 115) | The Sultanate of Oman | May 25, 1978 | Asia |
| 116) | The Socialist People's Libyan Arab Jamahiriya | Aug. 9, 1978 | Africa |
| 117) | The United States of America | Jan. 1, 1979 | North America |
| 118) | The Republic Djibouti | Jan. 8, 1979 | Africa |
| 119) | The Portuguese Republic | Feb. 8, 1979 | Europe |
| 120) | The Republic of Ireland | June 22, 1979 | Europe |
| 121) | The Republic of Ecuador | Jan. 2, 1980 | Latin America |
| 122) | The Republic of Colombia | Feb. 7, 1980 | Latin America |
| 123) | Zimbabwe | April 18, 1980 | Africa |
| 124) | The Republic of Kiribati | June 25, 1980 | Oceania |
| 125) | The Republic of Vanuatu | March 26, 1982 | Oceania |

| Name of Country | Date of Establishment of Relations | Location |
|---|---|---|
| 126) Antigua and Barbuda | Jan. 1, 1983 | Latin America |
| 127) The People's Republic of Angola | Jan. 12, 1983 | Africa |
| 128) The Republic of the Ivory Coast | March 2, 1983 | Africa |
| 129) The Kingdom of Lesotho | April 30, 1983 | Africa |

Notes I:

1) The Foreign Ministry of Ghana officially broke off diplomatic relations with China on October 20, 1966. The representatives from both countries signed a press communique to resume diplomatic relations on February 29, 1972.

2) The Chinese government closed the Chinese Embassy and broke off diplomatic relations with Zaire on September 18, 1961. On November 24, 1972, the two countries resumed diplomatic relations and dispatched diplomatic representatives at ambassadorial level to their respective countries.

3) The Prime Minister of Burundi presented a note to Chinese Ambassador proclaiming the temporary suspension of diplomatic relations of the two countries on January 29, 1965. The two countries resumed diplomatic relations at the ambassadorial level on October 13, 1971.

4) The Chinese Ministry of Foreign Affairs issued a statement closing the Chinese Embassy in Tunisia on September 26, 1967, which was reopened on October 8, 1971.

5) On January 6, 1966, the Central African Empire broke off diplomatic relations with China, but resumed relations and dispatched diplomatic representatives at the ambassadorial level to their respective countries on August 20, 1976.

6) On January 3, 1966, Benin announced the end of diplomatic relations with China, and resumed relations at the ambassadorial level on December 29, 1972.

7) San Marino established consular relations with China on May 6, 1971.

8) On June 17, 1954, China and Britain agreed to establish offices of Charge d'Affaires in their respective capitals, these were upgraded to ambassadorial level on March 13, 1972.

9) On November 19, 1954, China and the Netherlands agreed to establish offices of the Charge d'Affaires in their respective countries; these were upgraded to the ambassadorial level on May 18, 1972.

10) On February 22, 1973, China and the United States promulgated the Joint Communique and established liaison offices in their respective capitals. On January 1, 1979, formal diplomatic relations were established.

Note II:

1) On April 13, 1950, Indonesia established diplomatic relations with China. On October 23, 1967, Indonesia presented a note to China closing the Indonesian Embassy in China and requested China to close the Chinese Embassy and consulates in Indonesia. China protested on October 27. The two countries broke off diplomatic relations on October 31, 1967.

2) The Palestine Liberation Organization established an office in Beijing on March 22, 1965.

# A LIST OF CHINA'S WORLD RECORDS